FLYING ACES

FLYING ACES

AVIATION ART OF WORLD WAR II

James H. Kitchens

with an introduction by

Bernard C. Nalty

FRIEDMAN/FAIRFAX
PUBLISHERS

A FRIEDMAN/FAIRFAX BOOK

Friedman/Fairfax Publishers
15 West 26 Street
New York, NY 10010
Telephone (212) 685-6610
Fax (212) 685-1307
Please visit our website: www.metrobooks.com

Library of Congress Cataloging-in-Publication Data

Nalty, Bernard C.
    Flying aces : aviation art of World War II / Bernard C. Nalty and
James Kitchens.
      p.   cm.
    Includes bibliographical references and index.
    ISBN 1-56799-815-1
    1. World War, 1939–1945—Aerial operations Pictorial works.
    2. Airplanes, Military, in art.   I. Kitchens, James A.   II. Title.
    D785.N35 1999
    940.54'4--dc21   99-35932

Editor: Ann Kirby
Art Director: Kevin Ullrich
Photography Editor: Jennifer Bove
Production Manager: Camille Lee

Color separations by Bright Arts Graphics Pte. Ltd.
Printed in Singapore by KHL Printing Co. Pte. Ltd.

3 5 7 9 10 8 6 4 2

Distributed by Sterling Publishing Co., Inc.
387 Park Avenue South
New York, NY 10016-8810
Orders and customer service (800) 367-9692
Fax: (800) 542-7567
E-mail: custservice@sterlingpub.com
Website: www.sterlingpublishing.com

The author wishes to offer his very special and heartfelt thanks to Al Dodson
for his spiritual and material support, without which this book would never
have been completed. Warmest thanks also to Jim Perry, George Morrison,
Dr. Frank Olynyk, and John R. Beaman, Jr., who extended their friendly and
knowledgeable help with several obstinate items in the text.

The publisher gratefully acknowledges the many talented artists who allowed
their work to be included in these pages:

C. S. Bailey

Gil Cohen

Domenic DeNardo

James Dietz

Keith Ferris

Roy Grinnell

Jim Laurier

Mike Machat

Stan Stokes

Robert Taylor

Nicolas Trudgian

Special thanks also to Colin Heaton, whose personal archive of Flying Aces
photographs helped bring this book to life.

Contents

Introduction

The Point of the Spear

Bernard C. Nalty

On board the USS *Essex*, Maj. William A. Millington (center), USMC, goes over plans with his combined squads (VMF-123 and VMF-124) before a mission. Four Aces were produced by VMF-124, including Kenneth Ambrose Walsh, the first Corsair Ace.

IN THE FOUR DECADES THAT FOLLOWED THE FIRST SUCCESSFUL FLIGHT AT Kitty Hawk—in times of both peace and war—the airplane would make its mark on the national psyche, and the men who piloted them would become legends in their own time. By the time of the Second World War, the skies had become a primary battlefield, and the dogfights that ensued there between lone pilots occurred on a more deeply personal level than any battles that took place on the ground or elsewhere in the air. As brave airmen on both sides engaged in one-on-one combat high above the ground, their daring exploits captured the public imagination. While the Flying Aces tallied up their individual victories, their stories were recounted daily in newspapers and captured for astonished audiences in moviehouse newsreels.

In the years since, the stories of both Allied and Axis Aces have also proven inspirational to many talented artists. Working with historical photographs, documents, and through interviews with the pilots themselves, these gifted painters painstakingly recreate some of the war's most famous battles in vivid detail, and with staggering accuracy. This volume is a celebration of both the artists and the Aces and planes that have inspired them.

During World War II, a fighter pilot who destroyed five enemy aircraft in aerial combat earned, either officially or informally, the title of "ace". The type of military or naval aircraft shot down made no difference; the destruction of an unarmed transport counted as much as the downing of the enemy's deadliest fighter. The ace had to be a pilot—aerial gunners were no longer eligible, as they had been at times during World War I. The various air arms required confirmation of every victory, either by an eyewitness or by film from a movie camera synchronized to operate when the fighter's guns fired.

A problem arose when more than one pilot collaborated in destroying the same aircraft. In these instances, the American air services apportioned credit by awarding fractions of a victory to each of the pilots involved. Although the Soviet

Lt. John Thomas Blackburn's Fighting Squadron seventeen, VF-17, scored 154 victories flying the Vought F4U Corsair in the South Pacific. After operating from airfields ashore in the Solomon Islands, the squadron flew from the aircraft carrier USS *Bunker Hill*. Blackburn contributed eleven victories to the squadron's total.

Union, Italy, and the United Kingdom also recognized shared victories, other nations did not go so far in the interests of fairness and precise accounting. Germany's Luftwaffe, for example, awarded one victory per plane destroyed; the pilots who collaborated in the kill decided which of them would receive full credit. Similarly, the Japanese credited victories to flying units, which attributed them to individual pilots. The French followed a policy of awarding one victory to each pilot who contributed to a shared kill.

The question of conflicting claims troubled the Flying Tigers, the pilots of the American Volunteer Group, who were employed by the Chinese government against the Japanese invaders. An aerial melee over Kunming, China, on 29 December, 1941—three weeks after the Japanese attacked Pearl Harbor and some six months before the Flying Tigers disbanded—produced claims that all fifteen pilots involved had each downed at least one Japanese bomber in a formation of just ten. A squadron leader, Robert Sandell, accurately reported that the Flying Tigers had destroyed only three Japanese bombers, but a review panel decided that a fourth succumbed to battle damage and exploded en route back to its base. The fifteen pilots divided the four victories equally among them, each receiving 0.27 of a kill. A $500 bonus for every aerial victory no doubt contributed to a careful apportionment of credit that in a final accounting divided the bonuses for 294 victories among sixty-seven pilots. Individual scores ranged from 0.27 of a kill to the group's high of 15.55 by Robert Neale.

Although eyewitness testimony by pilots might be as accurate as Sandell's report of the dogfight over Kunming, the human eye could not establish the truth as accurately as the gun camera. For example, the aerial ambush on 18 April, 1943, that killed Adm. Isoroku Yamamoto, who had inspired the Japanese attack on Pearl Harbor, involved Lockheed P-38 Lightnings without gun cameras; the result was a lingering controversy over credit for shooting down the bomber that carried the admiral to his death. After the dangerous overwater mission, Capt. Thomas G. Lanphier claimed credit for downing one

LEFT: The Mitsubishi A6M (this one flown by Lt. Hideki Shingo, 5th Sentoi-Tai, IJN Shokaku) was known to Allied pilots as the Zero. Sacrificing armor for speed, Zeros were used with great success at the beginning of the war, but were eventually out-moded by newer Allied fighters. *Painting by C.S. Bailey*

bomber, which he came to believe had Yamamoto on board; 1st Lt. Besby F. Holmes claimed another bomber, and 1st Lt. Rex Barber claimed two. The reviewing authority awarded each of the pilots credit for shooting down one of three bombers, and there the matter rested until Japanese records that became available after the war revealed that the admiral and his party had traveled in just two bombers. An official review in the late 1960s concluded that Barber partici-pated with Lanphier in the destruction of one bomber and with Holmes in downing the other. This decision did not satisfy those who believed that Barber deserved credit for both kills. Their pressure resulted in another review in 1985 that ratified the earlier findings and thus failed to satisfy Barber's supporters, who continued to press their case, though without success.

Public fascination with aces like Neale and his fellow Flying Tigers—or Barber, Holmes, and Lanphier—originated in World War I at the outset of aerial combat. In those days, well-known prewar aviators emerged as the first heroes of aerial warfare. For example, the wartime exploits of the veteran French air-man Roland Garros soon matched his peacetime accomplishments. Garros, the first to fly across the Mediterranean from North Africa to France, shot down as many as six German planes, becoming the first pilot described as an "ace" by the press and his fellow fliers. His wartime career ended in April 1915 when he crash-landed and was taken prisoner.

Whereas other pioneers of aerial combat fired rifles or pistols or fixed machine guns atop the center section of a biplane's upper wing to fire outside the propeller arc, Garros armored his propeller with a strip of metal that deflected bullets fired from a machine gun fixed to the cowling ahead of the cockpit. This innovation betrayed him. The weight of the armor and the impact of bullets hitting it eventually damaged the balance of his propeller, set-ting up a vibration that forced him to shut down his engine and glide to a landing behind German lines.

Yet however crude, Garros' improvisation contributed much to the develop-ment of the fighter plane. It may well have inspired Anthony Fokker, a Dutch aeronautical engineer in the employ of the Germans, to devise an interrupter gear that synchronized the firing of a machine gun with the passage of the pro-peller in front of the muzzle. Fokker's universally copied idea—and the German fighter planes that he designed to use it—revolutionized aerial warfare and mul-tiplied the number of aces, who now could aim simply their airplanes at their targets and fire.

Numerous French aces surpassed Garros—men like René Fonck with seventy-five victories and Georges Guynémer with fifty-eight—and the govern-ment adopted a policy of publicizing individual pilots on the occasion of the their fifth victory and taking note of each subsequent kill. In the summer of 1917, as the number of aces escalated, the French high command stopped men-tioning pilots by name until they had won their tenth victory.

Germany awarded a decoration, *Pour le Mérite* (known commonly as the Blue Max) for a specific number of aerial victories, at first eight but ultimately twenty, and celebrated the accomplishments of successful fighter pilots like Oswald Boelcke, Max Immelmann, and Manfred von Richthofen. Boelcke, who downed forty victims, and Immelmann, who invented a maneuver—a half loop merging into a half roll—to reverse direction without sacrificing speed or altitude, flew the first of the Fokker aircraft fitted with the new interrupter gear and went on to more advanced fighters. With eighty aerial victories, von Richthofen, called "the Red Baron" from the color of his plane, became the ace of aces, even though he was killed in combat on 21 April, 1918, almost seven months before the war ended.

The British government proved reluctant to publicize individual airmen except when they received decorations, which rarely happened early in the war, and avoided official use of the term "Ace". The press and public ignored this policy, however, and celebrated a roster of Aces headed by Maj. Edward "Mick" Mannock with seventy-three victories. During World War I, the concept of the Ace took root, even in Great Britain, to flourish in the next major conflict.

World War II began with small cadres of professional military pilots, rather than aerial adventurers, in the fighter forces of the major belligerents. The German contingent included future Aces like Erich Hartmann, Johannes Steinhoff, and Dietrich Hrabak, who had become military aviators before Adolf Hitler attacked Poland on 1 September, 1939. Indeed, Hrabak, who went on to score 125 victories, was shot down on the first day of the war.

Unique among the veteran airmen was Britain's Douglas R. S. Bader, who suffered the loss of both legs as the result of a crash in 1931. Although fitted with artificial legs that enabled him to continue flying, he received a medical discharge from the Royal Air Force. When Britain and France went to war on behalf of Poland, his services were needed. Bader helped win the Battle of Britain in 1940 and downed twenty-two German aircraft before being shot down over German-occupied France and taken prisoner in August of the following year.

By the time the Japanese attacked Pearl Harbor in December 1941, plunging the United States into World War II, an emergency expansion of the Army Air Corps, along with Navy and Marine Corps aviation, had already begun. During the spring and summer of 1941, with the blessing of federal authorities, recruiters for the American Volunteer Group signed contracts with a hundred veteran pilots, not all of whom had flown fighters. Indeed, a Navy dive-bomber pilot, Robert Neale, became the highest scorer of the Flying Tigers. When the group disbanded, another Flying Tiger, Gregory Boyington, returned to the Marine Corps, where he became its leading Ace with twenty-eight victories and earned the Medal of Honor, the highest American award for valor. James Howard, recruited from the Navy for the American Volunteer Group, accepted a commission in the Army Air Corps and earned the Medal of Honor on 11 January, 1944, for single-handedly breaking up an attack on a

RIGHT: The Grumman F4F-3 "Wildcat" (this one flown by Lt. Edward "Butch" O'Hare, VF, USS *Lexington*) was the U.S. Navy's primary fighter until it was replaced by the F-4U Corsair and the F-6F Hellcat.

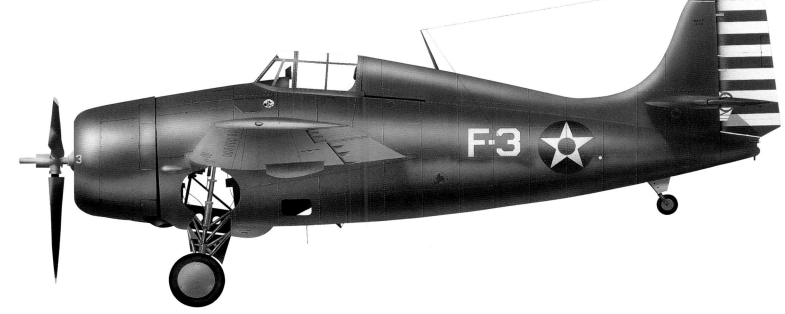

formation of B-17s bombing an aircraft factory at Oschersleben, Germany.

Fighter Aces again captured the imagination of the public, whether these airmen were Flying Tigers—American volunteers who fought for China before the United States went to war—or others like them. These pilots seemed the embodiment of the fliers of fiction, who took off at dawn, a joke on their lips, to risk a fiery death. Hollywood and the pulp magazines had turned the Ace—an individual mixture of ambition and selflessness, fear and courage, science and superstition—into a knight of the sky, whose virtues inspired awe and whose occasional failings deserved understanding and forgiveness.

A group of knights like these, had they actually existed, could not have met the demands of a conflict that was expanding geographically while its weapons became ever more complex. As in World War I, the belligerents had to mass-produce airmen, creating a succession of Aces until victory was won. The United States had the most success in training the fliers it needed, even though its armed forces demanded higher scores on the general classification test and better physical condition for air cadets than for persons

Gen. Hannes Trautloft, also known as "the father of the JG 54 Green Hearts," earned fifty-eight aerial victories for Luftwaffe, a record that earned him the Knight's Cross.

assigned to other combat branches. The American air services adjusted standards, as well as subjects and schedules, when necessary to ensure adequate numbers of pilots would be available on time. For example, when college training seemed a stumbling block, the Army Air Forces began recruiting high school graduates to train as sergeant pilots, who later might become warrant officers or commissioned officers. One highly successful graduate of the program was Charles E. "Chuck" Yeager, who described himself as a "D History student from Hamlin High," West Virginia. Yeager earned a commission during the war, became a fighter Ace, broke the so-called sound barrier with the rocket-powered Bell X-1 in 1947, and retired as a general officer.

The successful American pilot training program benefitted from an aircraft industry, safe from hostile attack, that turned out tens of thousands of training planes for the United States and its allies. The supply of fuel for flight training continued without interruption, and the number of installations kept pace with demand, as land that had grown corn or cotton in 1941 soon produced a harvest of pilots instead.

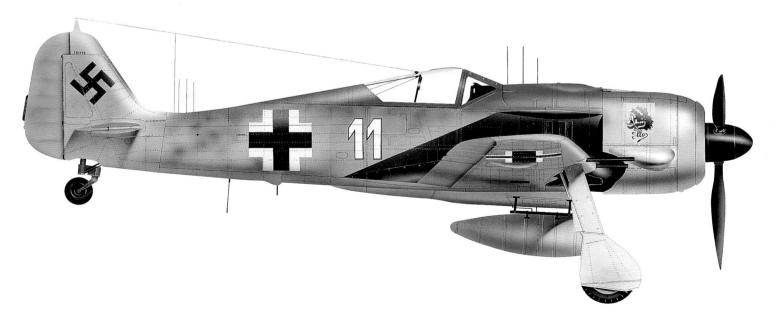

LEFT: The Focke-Wulf FW 190A (this one flown by Oberlietnant Fritz Krause, UNJGr10) was one of Germany's deadliest fighter planes. *Painting by C.S. Bailey.*

RIGHT: The North American P51B Mustang was probably the best fighter of World War II, serving the Eighth Air Force in large numbers from late in 1943 through the end of the war. This plane was flown by ace Duane W. Beeson of the Eighth Air Force, 4th Fighter Group, who closed out the war with more than seventeen victories. *Painting by C.S. Bailey.*

The United Kingdom tapped the resources of the British Commonwealth to create and replenish its corps of fighter pilots. Thus did A. G. "Sailor" Malan of South Africa, who entered the Royal Air Force in 1936 and scored thirty-two aerial victories, fight alongside James E. "Johnnie" Johnson, a native of the British Isles, who started training as World War II began and won thirty-eight confirmed victories. Canada played a critical role in maintaining the wartime strength of the Royal Air Force. Besides deploying a fighter unit in time for the Battle of Britain, Canada operated 360 wartime training fields that produced bomber crews as well as fighter pilots.

Both Japan and Germany failed to plan for a long war. Adolf Hitler expected to conquer the Soviet Union as swiftly as he had overrun western Europe, and Japanese leaders, despite a warning from Admiral Yamamoto of hard fighting to come, believed the United States would lose heart after its early defeats and accept Japanese domination of the western Pacific. Unceasing attrition and a shortage of gasoline prevented these nations from making the kind of massive training effort that might have compensated for the errors in planning.

Too many Japanese pilots perished in naval battles like Midway or the Philippine Sea, died in New Guinea, the Solomons, or the Marianas, or languished on islands bypassed by the advancing Americans. American submarines and minefields cut the convoy route that brought oil from the conquered Netherlands East Indies to Japan. As fuel supplies diminished, Japan could

no longer invest hundreds of hours of flying time to teach pilots to fight and survive. As defeat drew closer, Japan could offer its new pilots only enough training for suicide missions against the United States fleet.

More than five years of attrition in aerial battles fought from the skies over Britain, North Africa, and the Soviet Union depleted the ranks of German fighter pilots. The strategic bombing of the oil industry, and the Soviet capture of the Romanian oil fields and refineries, crippled pilot training. When German factories began producing revolutionary jet fighters, albeit in small numbers, the Luftwaffe had to turn to the survivors of earlier battles—veterans like Georg-Peter Eder and Johannes Steinhoff—to fly them.

World War II reaffirmed the legend of the fighter Ace, thanks to the exploits of pilots like Erich Hartmann of Germany, Johnnie Johnson of Great Britain, Saburo Sakai of Japan, I. N. Kozhedub of the Soviet Union, and Americans like Richard Bong, Thomas McGuire, and David McCampbell. But the Second World War also demonstrated that the gallant and colorful fighter ace represented the gleaming point on a spear fashioned by thousands of people. The defeat of Germany and Japan revealed that the Ace depended not only on his own sharply honed skills but also on the support of his fellow pilots and mechanics, on the training establishment that shaped him, and on the national economic and industrial base that provided him with a fighter plane, fuel, and munitions.

Against the Tide

Pierre Le Gloan, *L'Armée de l'air*

Stan Stokes

I<small>T IS MID</small>-J<small>UNE</small> 1940. C<small>ANOPY OPENED FOR MAXIMUM VISIBILITY, ENGINE</small> throttled back, *Sergent-Chef* Pierre Le Gloan of *Group de chasse* III/6 escorts two Bloch MB.210s and a Bréguet Bré.693 south, away from the German forces raging into northern France. Below him, the City of Light is just a few days away from three years of Nazi occupation, and *Serg.-Ch.* Le Gloan may well be taking what will be his last look at the ever-familar Notre Dame cathedral, Eiffel Tower, and beautiful Seine bridges.

Born at Kergrist-Moëlou (Côtes-du-Nord) in 1913, Le Gloan enlisted in the French Air Force in 1931. He entered fighter training in 1933 and by 1939 had risen to *Sergent-Chef*, or master sergeant, with the GC III/6. At the outbreak of the war, the unit was equipped with the Morane-Saulnier MS.406, and it was with a MS.406 that Le Gloan won his first aerial victory, a Dornier Do 17, on 23 November, 1939.

At the end of May 1940, GC III/6 re-equipped with the Dewoitine D.520, the best fighter the French Air Force had, and Le Gloan used it to run his certain victories up to eleven by mid-June. Following the fall of France, he fled with his unit to North Africa, where he served with Vichy forces in the Levant and claimed several RAF Hawker Hurricanes. After the fall of North Africa, Le Gloan, now a *Lieutenant*, went over to Free French forces as squadron commander in the GC III/6, now rebaptized *Roussillon*. He died on 11 September 1943, in a flaming belly landing near Mostaganem, Algeria, following sudden engine failure in his P-39 Aircobra. At the time his victory score stood at eighteen, plus three probables.

Stung by the Wasp

Reade F. Tilley, RAF and USAF

Stan Stokes

MALTA IS A SMALL ROCKY ISLAND THAT RISES OUT OF THE NARROWS between Sicily and the Tunisian coast, a place of great strategic worth, because of its position between the eastern and western Mediterranean. The British, governors of Malta for centuries, clung doggedly to the little island after the Mediterranean became an Axis lake in 1941, and they were still holding it late in the year, despite incessant and ferocious German air attacks from Sicily. By April 1942, however, the island's air defenses were down to twenty to thirty fighters, and its situation was desperate. Reinforcement was imperative, but how to do it when the Axis owned the sea and skies?

To relieve Malta, Winston Churchill turned to President Roosevelt with a bold request: since British carriers were inadequate or unavailable, would the U.S. Navy allow its big carrier USS *Wasp* to bring a load of fighters as close as possible, then fly them off on a one-way delivery? Roosevelt generously replied in the affirmative, and on 12–13 April, 1942, the *Wasp* took on fifty-two Spitfire Mk Vcs fitted with slipper tanks at Glasgow. During the night of 19–20 April she sneaked to within 620 miles (992km) of Malta and just at dawn on the 20th sent off forty-seven Spitfires from Nos. 601 and 603 squadrons, of which forty-six arrived safely.

American Reade F. Tilley, then a pilot officer in No. 601 "County of London" Squadron, was part of the *Wasp*'s April sting. Born in Florida in 1918, Tilley had enlisted in the RCAF in 1940 and was sent to England, where he served first with No. 121 "Eagle" Squadron and then with No. 601 Squadron. He finished the war with seven confirmed air victories and retired from the USAF as a colonel in 1971.

WING COMMANDER JOHN EDGAR "JOHNNIE" JOHNSON

Johnnie Johnson began learning to fly as a civilian, entered the Royal Air Force as a "sergeant pilot under training," graduated, received a commission, and joined a squadron in the spring of 1940. While a member of a fighter wing commanded by Douglas Bader, he scored his first aerial victory, destroying a Messerschmitt Me 109. Johnson flew various models of the Spitfire as he became the leading British ace in numbers of confirmed victories, claiming his thirty-eight and final victim over the Rhine on 27 September, 1944. Another Royal Air Force pilot, Marmaduke T. St. John Pattle of South Africa, may well have downed forty or more aircraft, but the records of his squadron were lost in the spring of 1941 when the British withdrew from Greece, where Pattle himself was killed.

Eagle's Prey

No. 71 "Eagle" Squadron, RAF

Robert Taylor

ROBERT TAYLOR'S *EAGLES PREY* COMMEMORATES THE AMERICANS WHO volunteered for service in the Royal Air Force before the United States itself went to war in 1941. Ultimately there were sufficient American volunteers to constitute three so-called "Eagle" fighter squadrons, No. 71, No. 121, and No. 133. Of the three, No. 71 was the firstborn, being organized in September 1940. Initially equipped with Hawker Hurricane IIas, the squadron re-equipped with Supermarine Spitfire Mk IIas, then with Mk Vbs, in August 1941. Its home airfield at the time was RAF Station North Weald in the 11th Group area. During 1941, No. 71 Squadron was, like much of Fighter Command, primarily engaged in Rodeos, Circuses, and Rhubarbs over northern France, missions intended to bait the Luftwaffe for battle and keep it off balance. The unit took its Spitfires to Martlesham Heath in December 1941, then in May 1942 transferred yet again to RAF Station Debden. With the USAAF presence in England growing mightily, No. 71 Squadron was transferred to the Eighth Air Force on 29 September, 1942, becoming 334th Fighter Squadron of the 4th Fighter Group.

At the end of its RAF service, No. 71 "Eagle" Squadron had achieved forty-one aerial victories. *Eagles Prey* portrays one of those victories, a Bf 109G-2 lying on its belly in northern France while two Spitfire Mk Vbs circle overhead.

Flying Tigers
American Volunteer Group (AVG)

Stan Stokes

IN LATE 1941 AND EARLY 1942, THE AMERICAN VOLUNTEER GROUP (AVG) provided about the only cheery war headlines for Americans numbed and humiliated by events in Hawaii and Asia. Formed in 1941 to bolster Chiang Kai-shek's Nationalist Chinese air force, the Group comprised 240 American volunteers—100 of them pilots—recruited by the shadowy, semi-official Central Aircraft Manufacturing Company (CAMCO). The operation was the brainchild of Claire L. Chennault, a driving, craggy-faced, ex–Air Corps fighter advocate and advisor to Chiang Kai-shek. Formed into three squadrons equipped with Curtiss P-40Cs scrounged from a British order, Chennault's "Flying Tigers" went into action over Burma on 20 December 1941. Over the next six months, the AVG claimed—and was paid for—294 Japanese aircraft downed. This total is somewhat controversial, but the debate over its accuracy perhaps misses the point—the AVG gave Americans pride and hope amid the tears and fears of early 1942.

The American Volunteer Group, nicknamed the "Flying Tigers," defended southwestern China against Japan even prior to the bombing of Pearl Harbor. After the group disbanded in July 1942, many fliers enlisted in the U.S. Army Air Forces.

Tiger Claws

Kenneth Jernstedt, AVG

Stan Stokes

KENNETH JERNSTEDT WAS AMONG THE ONE HUNDRED AMERICAN PILOTS recruited in 1941 to fly for the American Volunteer Group (AVG) as part of Chiang Kai-shek's Nationalist Chinese Air Force. Following his graduation from Linfield College in 1939, Jernstedt had enlisted in the U.S. Navy's aviation program. When representatives of the Central Aircraft Manufacturing Company (CAMCO)—the front for Claire Chennault's "Special Air Unit"—offered him big money and a patriotic adventure, however, Jernstedt signed their contract. In return for $600 a month in salary plus $500 for each Japanese plane downed, he agreed to one year's service as the equivalent of a lieutenant with CAMCO, "an aircraft manufacturing, operating and repair business in China," to "perform such duties as the Employer may direct." There was no mention of combat, cockpit time, exact service conditions, or even bonuses, though all these were plain between the lines.

Arriving in Burma in August 1941, Jernstedt went through Chennault's standard three-month course on how to swat Japanese airplanes and survive: seventy-two hours of lecture and sixty hours of flight training in tactics, gunnery, and above all, the pluses and minuses of the AVG's Curtiss P-40C Tomahawk. Then came combat. Assigned aircraft no. 88 in the 3rd Pursuit Squadron—the "Hell's Angels"—Jernstedt racked up his first claim on Christmas Day, 25 December, 1941, when he shot down a Nakajima Ki 43 Hayabusa fighter from the 64th *Sentai* close to Rangoon. By the time the AVG was disbanded in July 1942, he had earned 10.5 victories. Back home in Hood River, Oregon, Jernstedt's banker told him that he knew he was doing all right "because the money kept coming in."

Defiant but Doomed

Adolf Galland, Luftwaffe

Stan Stokes

THE DEFIANT WAS THE LAST IN A SERIES OF BOULTON-PAUL FIGHTER designs for the RAF that stretched back to 1918. None of the company's aircraft had achieved large contracts or great renown, but in the mid-thirties the firm thought it finally had a winner with the Defiant, a unique two-seater whose punch consisted solely of four .303 machine guns in a power-operated turret. Presumably, the Defiant's gunner was to coach his pilot about how to maneuver while trying to bring his guns to bear—with the clarity of hindsight, a decidedly wrong-headed concept that was doomed to failure. Nonetheless, the RAF, desperate for fighters in the late 1930s, bought several hundred Defiants, and some of these found their way to No. 264 Squadron during the Battle of Britain.

Early on 28 August, 1940, twelve Defiants of No. 264 Squadron lifted off from Hornchurch to intercept a Luftwaffe raid over the white cliffs of Dover. No doubt their crews were apprehensive as they searched the morning skies for any sign of trouble, for over the previous four days, the squadron had lost seven aircraft and nine air crew in combat. Just before 0900, British fears turned into a nightmare when the Defiants tangled with twenty-seven He 111s from KG 53. Two Defiants had already turned away damaged when the other ten were hit by a slashing attack from the crack JG 26 *Schlageter* fighter wing led by its commander and four-time ace Adolph Galland. JG 26's Messerschmitts quickly shot down three Defiants—one credited to Galland—and damaged another. This one-sided fight proved to be the turret fighter's swan song, for a few days later it was permanently withdrawn from daylight operations. A few soldiered on into 1941 as night fighters, but with little effect and no affection from their pilots.

Legendary Luftwaffe fighter pilot Adolf Galland finished the war with no fewer than 104 aerial victories. One of those wins came in a heated battle that took down three Defiants, and eventually led to that plane's demise.

Bader's Bus Company

Douglas R. S. Bader, RAF

Robert Taylor

HEROISM IS NOT NECESSARILY EXCEPTIONAL BRAVERY UNDER FIRE; IT CAN also be found in a determined resolve to overcome the slings and arrows of life. Heroism of each kind abounds, but seldom indeed does one find both types in the same individual. Group Captain Douglas R. S. Bader was such a man.

After graduation from the RAF College at Cranwell in September 1928, Bader had been posted to No. 23 Squadron flying Gloster Gamecocks from RAF Station Kenley. Off duty, he expressed his pluck, grit, and zest for life in playing for several rugby and cricket teams. Then, on 14 December, 1931, Bader's vibrant and vital lifestyle was shattered when his Bristol Bulldog fighter smashed into the ground during aerobatics practice. Pulled from the pile of twisted metal and fabric, the semiconscious pilot was rushed to hospital, where both of his legs were amputated, one above the knee. After weeks of lingering on death's doorstep, the young pilot was finally released for therapy and fitted with artificial limbs.

At age twenty-two, Bader had to make a fresh start. Invalided out of the RAF in 1933, he worked at a ground job in Shell Petroleum's aviation department. But Bader was obsessed; he believed he could still fly, and with war approaching, the RAF gave him a chance to prove it. In 1939 he went back into uniform, refreshed himself on training aircraft, and in early 1940, went operational with No. 19 Squadron (Spitfires). By July he was a squadron commander; a year later he had eighteen victories, wore the DFC and DSO, and commanded the Tangmere Wing (call sign "Bader's Bus Company"). Shot down in August 1941, he survived as a POW, made a distinguished post-war career, and was knighted in 1976. He died of a heart attack on 5 September, 1982, an exceptional leader and an inspirational example of fortitude and valor.

Despite a handicap, Douglas Bader finished off the war with a formidable record. It is said Adolf Galland himself allowed a new pair of metal legs to be parachuted in for the POW after Bader's artificial limbs were damaged during his escape landing.

Too Little, Too Late

20th Pursuit Squadron, USAAF

Keith Ferris

CONCEALED IN KEITH FERRIS' PORTRAYAL OF A USAAF P-40B WHEELING against three Japanese A6M5 Model 21 Zero fighters over Clark Field, the Philippines, is a dynamic warning of what can happen when a nation lets its defenses down. Woefully underfunded, understrength, and underestimated throughout the 1920s and 1930s, the Army Air Forces had just five fighter squadrons—ninety aircraft at best—available to defend the Philippines when the Japanese struck on 8 December, 1941. Two of these squadrons were barely combat-ready, having been assigned their aircraft the day before the attack. And the performance of the American P-40Bs, P-40Es, and P-35s left much to be desired as well.

Despite their inadequate materiel and lack of any combat experience, pilots from the 20th Pursuit Squadron fought back valiantly when fifty-two Mitsubishi G4M Betty bombers escorted by thirty-six A6M5 Zeroes appeared over Clark Field at 1220 on 8 December. Though every advantage lay with the enemy, Lt. Joseph H. Moore, the 20th's squadron commander, managed to lead two other P-40Bs into the air. In a series of swirling one-sided dogfights, the Americans made three claims, the first enemy aircraft to be shot down over the Philippines. Against these victories, the Japanese destroyed ten U.S. fighters at Clark by bombing or strafing, and elsewhere the picture was the same. Overall, it was a dismal, ignominious day for United States' arms—the nation had yet to learn the bitter lesson that the highest valor is no substitute for being prepared.

Christmas Over Rangoon

American Volunteer Group (AVG)

Roy Grinnell

For the three squadrons of Claire Chennault's American Volunteer Group, Christmas Day, 1941, was a day little different from any in the preceding week. Having gone into combat for the first time on 20 December, the Americans were now beginning to get the feel of their aircraft, a shaky early warning system, Burma's 100-degree F (38°C) weather, the banyan trees, and the face of the Japanese enemy.

On their side, the Japanese had become well aware of the obnoxious American presence around Rangoon and were determined to rid themselves of it. On 25 December they mounted a massive raid—ninety-eight Mitsubishi Ki 21 medium bombers in two waves, escorted by more than fifty Nakajima Ki 27s and Ki 43s headed for the city proper and nearby Mingladon Airfield. Despite inadequate warning, a half-dozen P-40Cs of the 1st Pursuit Squadron ("Adam and Eve") accompanied by sixteen RAF Buffaloes managed to fall on the first wave and break it up. Using Chennault's prescribed "no dogfighting" tactics, Flt. Ldrs. Tom Haywood and Charley Older (P-40C no. 68) each claimed two bombers, while Flt. Ldrs. Duke Hedman and George McMillan claimed three apiece. By this time, other Flying Tigers from the 3rd Pursuit Squadron ("Hell's Angels") joined what had become a mad melee of howling engines, chattering machine guns, and flaming debris scattered across miles of Burma sky. When the dust settled at the end of the day, the Flying Tigers submitted rather optimistic claims for twenty-four Japanese planes destroyed, two probables, and six damaged. The AVG had lost two P-40s, but both pilots later turned up unhurt. Christmas Day, 1941, had scarcely been a day of peace on earth, but it had left the Japanese intentions for Rangoon badly shaken.

Maple Leaf Scramble

No. 1 Squadron, RCAF

Robert Taylor

IN 1940, THE SUPERMARINE SPITFIRE WAS THE AERONAUTICAL IDOL OF the English people, who rightly and proudly believed Reginald Mitchell's creation to be without peer as a defender of the realm. The passage of time has tended to amplify the aura of glamor and glory around the Spitfire's role in the Battle of Britain, virtually creating the legend that it was the Spitfire that saved England in 1940. This impression, however, is only partially supported. While it is certainly true that the Hawker Hurricane lacked some of the good looks, modernity, and performance of the Spitfire, it had its own virtues, including good maneuverability, ruggedness, stability, and easy repair. Most importantly, however, the Hurricane was available in numbers in 1940: Chief Air Marshal Hugh Dowding, chief of Fighter Command, had two Hurricanes for every Spitfire in his order of battle. Whenever possible, Dowding's group commanders and their fighter controllers tried to maximize their assets by vectoring Hurricane squadrons onto Luftwaffe bomber formations, while more capable Spitfires were set on the fighter escorts. In practice, however, these tactics were not always possible, and Hurricane pilots had to deal with whatever unfolded in the summer skies of 1940.

Robert Taylor's *Maple Leaf Scramble* honors No. 1 Squadron of the Royal Canadian Air Force, which flew Hurricanes throughout the hard days of August and September 1940. A permanent unit of the RCAF, No. 1 Squadron had brought its own Hurricanes to England in June 1940. After preparation of the aircraft and a period of operational training, No.1 Squadron went into action with No. 11 Group from RAF Station Northholt, on the western outskirts of London. During late August and early September, the unit was continually scrambled off to defend the capital, and casualties were heavy. By the beginning of October, the squadron was essentially depleted, and on 11 October it was withdrawn to Scotland. In February 1941, it moved to Yorkshire and on 1 March, 1941, was redesignated No. 401 Squadron.

Birth of a Legend

Saburo Sakai, IJNAF

Stan Stokes

ABOUT STAN STOKES' *BIRTH OF A LEGEND*, ONE MIGHT WELL ASK, *which* legend? The painting represents a rare moment that spawned not one but two aviation legends, an attack by Saburo Sakai of the Imperial Japanese Navy on an Army Air Forces B-17 flown by Capt. Colin Kelly.

Three days after Pearl Harbor, with the defenses of the Philippines crumbling all around, Capt. Kelly took one of the few surviving B-17s from Clark Field on a mission to bomb an aircraft carrier reported off Luzon. Finding no carrier, he bombed and apparently badly damaged what at the time was thought to be the battleship *Haruna*. Returning to Clark Field, Kelly's B-17 was attacked and badly shot up by Zeroes, one of them flown by NAP 1/C Saburo Sakai. After his crew bailed out, Kelly attempted to force-land his crippled bomber but failed and was killed in the ensuing crash. Desperate for any good news at this dark hour, Allied press reports seized on the sinking of the Japanese ship and turned it into a triumph of American arms. Capt. Kelly was posthumously awarded the Distinguished Service Cross for sinking the vessel (which has never been conclusively identified, but was not the *Haruna*), and immediately became America's first air war hero.

After the fight with Kelly's B-17, Saburo Sakai went on to become one of Japan's leading World War II fighter aces. Despite losing an eye over Guadalcanal in August 1942, he continued to fly, survived more than two-hundred air combats with sixty-four victories, and became a legend in the annals of fighter pilots. After the war he co-authored a highly successful history of the Zero fighter that he had helped make famous (*Zero!* with Martin Caidin, 1961).

Shortly after the bombing of Pearl Harbor Capt. Colin Kelly (below) died in action in the Phillipines, shot down by a swarm of Japanese Zeros, among them one piloted by the soon-to-be legendary Saburo Sakai (left). Sakai finished the war with sixty-four victories, while Kelly—one of the first American fighter casualties of World War II—was awarded the Distinguished Service Cross posthumously.

Holding the Line

No. 111 "Treble One" Squadron, RAF

Nicolas Trudgian

THE RAF HAS TRADITIONALLY DOWNPLAYED THE ROLE OF THE INDIVIDUAL within a unit and of units within the service, preferring to emphasize larger elements and values. Even had this been otherwise, however, most fighter squadrons during the Battle of Britain performed at a remarkably similar and usually exemplary level. Singling out No. 111 ("Treble One") Squadron as exceptional, therefore, risks creating a misperception. Nonetheless, in August 1940, the squadron took on a special challenge, to which it responded with distinction.

On 18 August, 1940, the day that Alfred Price has called the hardest of the Battle of Britain, the Luftwaffe threw the book at the RAF's airfields and radar stations, launching a one-hundred–plus plane raid against RAF Stations Kenley, West Malling, and North Weald; Ford Naval Air Station; Poling radar station; and other targets. The 9. *Staffel* of KG 76 with Dornier Do 17Zs was assigned RAF Kenley, and it executed a savage low-level attack on the aerodrome with nine Dorniers at 0122. Ground fire damaged several Do 17Zs, but on the way out, 9./KG 76 also ran into No. 111 Squadron's Hurricanes out of Croydon, who harried them unmercifully at tree-top level. By the time it was all over, two Dorniers had crashed in England, two had ditched in the Channel, and the remaining five had all returned shot to pieces, some flown back carrying their dead pilots.

Nicolas Trudgian's painting captures "Treble One" mauling one of the Kenley raiders, *Fw.* Reichel's Do 17Z-3 F1 + CT, which staggered back on one engine to crash-land at Abbeville with a wounded gunner and 60 percent damage. On its side, No. 111 Squadron lost a pilot and three Hurricanes, but it had held the line with honor on the hardest day in the Battle of Britain.

Height of the Battle

No. 74 "Tiger" Squadron, RAF

Robert Taylor

ROBERT TAYLOR'S MAGNIFICENT *HEIGHT OF THE BATTLE* REPRESENTS A scene repeated many times over England between early August and mid-September 1940, the crucial period of the Battle of Britain. The howl of Rolls-Royce Merlins and the bass of droning Junkers Jumos sounds an ominous polyphony in the heavens as a flight of Spitfire Mk Is from No. 74 "Tiger" Squadron peels off in pairs out of the sun—note the shadows on Spitfire ZP-S—to dive on a large formation of He 111s below. Very soon Browning .303s and Rhein-Metall Borsig MG 15s will add their staccato counterpoint to the ballet, men and machines will die, and the dance with death will go on until the bombers retreat to France.

No. 74 "Tiger" Squadron, first constituted in 1917, was disbanded in 1919. Reformed in 1935, the squadron initially received Gloster Gauntlets, which it exchanged for Supermarine Spitfire Mk Is in February 1939. During July and early August 1940, No. 74 Squadron operated out of RAF Station Hornchurch as part of Air Vice-Marshal Keith Park's 11 Group. Badly battle-worn, it was withdrawn to Air Vice-Marshal Trafford Leigh-Mallory's 12 Group airfields at Wittering, Kirton-in-Lindsey, and Coltishall. In 1940, the unit's most notable pilot was undoubtedly Adolf G. "Sailor" Malan, an aggressive, highly experienced flyer who became the squadron leader on 8 August 1940. At that point Malan had thirteen victories and several shared kills. His *10 Rules of Air Fighting* was written at Kirton-in-Lindsey in late August–early September 1940 and distributed throughout Fighter Command, no doubt saving some pilots' lives, and increasing others' effectiveness.

Tiger Fire
American Volunteer Group (AVG)

Nicolas Trudgian

NICOLAS TRUDGIAN'S *TIGER FIRE* REPRESENTS A SOMEWHAT FANCIFUL AIR combat scene set in southern Burma in early 1942, when the region's air defense rested on fewer than one hundred Curtiss P-40Cs of the American Volunteer Group and just one squadron (No. 67) of RAF Brewster Buffaloes. Sweeping low over the lush tropical landscape, Charley Older in P-40C no. 68 leads four other P-40Cs from the AVG's 3rd Pursuit Squadron (the "Hell's Angels") full-bore at low altitude after a lone Japanese Mitsubishi A6M2 Model 21 Zero, which they seem to have boxed in.

Artist Trudgian has beautifully captured the adrenalin and howling engines, but a combat scenario with odds of five-to-one for the Flying Tigers would have been rare indeed, since Chennault's squadrons were almost always heavily out-numbered. Although commonly reported by the Allies, the Zero, the Imperial Navy's best carrier-based fighter, seldom, if ever, appeared over Burma; Japanese Army fighters such as Nakajima's Ki 27 Nate, Ki 43 Oscar, and Ki 44 Tojo were probably mistaken for Zeroes. Finally, the American pilots would have been in for a dressing-down after their combat reports were filed, because AVG commander Claire Chennault would never have approved of so many of his precious aircraft chasing one Japanese at such low altitude!

Maj. John R. Alison was one of many pilots who served with the AAF China Air Task Force, which took over the Flying Tigers' bases and planes after the AVG disbanded. As part of the CATF's 23rd FG, Alison was credited with six aerial victories.

Italian Air Stallion

Adriano Visconti, *Regia Aeronautica* and *Aeronautica Nazionale Repubblicana*

Stan Stokes

ITALIAN UNITS, PERSONNEL, OPERATIONS, AND ACHIEVEMENTS ARE perhaps the least known of all the major World War II combatants. Even today, the history of the *Regia Aeronautica* (RA) and the *Aeronautica Nazionale Repubblicana* (ANR) remains underexplored and somewhat foggy, and as new information continues to turn up, the careers of some Italian flyers will be subject to clarification or revision. This has already been the case with *Magg.* Adriano Visconti.

Little is known of Visconti's career. Once credited with twenty-six aerial victories and traditionally regarded as Italy's leading ace of World War II, his own logbooks show that he properly should be credited with six victories with the

RA and four with the *ANR*. According to current tabulations, his score of ten would place him forty-seventh among Italian pilots with air victories.

Visconti served with the 7° *Gruppo*, which fought as a day fighter unit with Macchi MC.200s in Italy and Sicily from 1940 to 1943. After Italy surrendered in September 1943, he continued in service with the *ANR*, a German proxy air force operating in northern Italy. As an *ANR* pilot during 1944 and early 1945 Visconti flew one of Italy's best wartime fighters, the Macchi MC.205 *Veltro* ("Greyhound") with the 1° *Gruppo di caccia*. Amid the civil disorder and settling of scores that characterized the end of the war in Italy, *Magg.* Visconti was put to death by partisans in Milan on 29 April, 1945.

Forgotten Hero

Marmaduke T. St. John "Pat" Pattle, RAF

Stan Stokes

BORN IN SOUTH AFRICA IN 1912, MARMADUKE T. ST. JOHN "PAT" PATTLE joined the South African Air Force after college. Turned down for flight training, he went to England in 1936, where he joined the RAF and entered pilot training. He was assigned to No. 80 Squadron and went with it to Egypt in 1938.

For the first several months of the war, Pattle's unit saw little action until Benito Mussolini's forces swarmed into North Africa. No. 80 Squadron's outnumbered and outdated Gladiators were soon hotly engaged over Libya, where Pattle claimed his first two victories, a Breda Br.65 and a FIAT CR.42, on 4 August, 1940. Before the end of the year, he had claimed several more CR.42s and damaged three CANT Z.1007bis trimotor bombers, no easy prey for the Gloster biplane.

In November, No. 80 Squadron moved north to Greece; Pattle brought his score to 20-plus over the Aegean and Peloponnesus. When his unit finally obtained Hurricanes on 20 February, 1941, the new aircraft unleashed all of Pattle's flying and fighting gifts. During the next thirty-nine days, he shot down no fewer than twenty-six enemy aircraft, nine of them Bf 109Es. On 20 April, 1941, the odds caught up with the brave South African. While attempting to save a squadron mate, Pattle was shot down and killed by a Bf 110 from 5./ZG 26 over Eleusis Bay. His final score is debatable, but those who served with him insist it should be over forty, which if true would make him the leading British ace of World War II.

Buffalo Ace

Eino I. Juuttilainen and the Brewster Buffalo

Stan Stokes

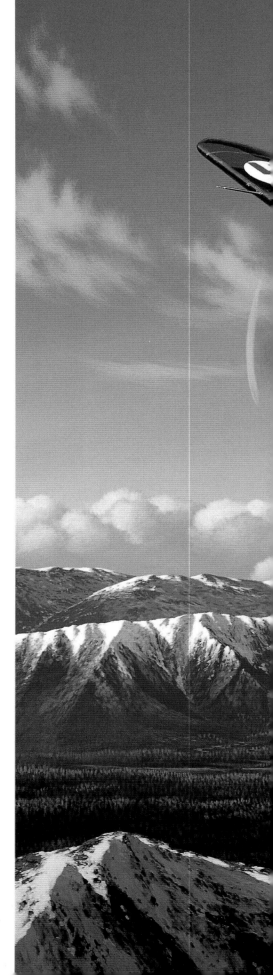

THE BREWSTER F2A BUFFALO WAS ORIGINALLY DESIGNED IN THE LATE 1930s as a U.S. Navy fighter, and in 1939–1940 it became the first monoplane to operate in any numbers from aircraft carriers. By 1941, updated Buffaloes could be found serving the U.S. Navy and Marines in the Pacific, the Royal Air Force in Burma, and the Royal Netherlands Air Force in Indonesia. The Buffalo, unfortunately, was an underachiever, and combat against modern Japanese fighters flown by aggressive pilots mercilessly exposed all of its deficiencies. By mid-1942, the airplane was an unlamented thing of the past in U.S., RAF, and Dutch inventories.

In contrast to its failure in the Pacific, however, the Buffalo achieved marked success with the *Suomen Ilmavoimien* (Finnish air forces), which snapped up forty-three declared surplus and released for export by the U.S. Navy in 1940. The Finns, then confronting the Russian bear on their southern and eastern flanks, immediately distributed the Buffaloes to frontline squadrons, among them LeVv 24. During the next three years, Finnish Buffalo pilots conclusively proved that good training, *esprit de corps*, experience, valor, and a need to defend one's homeland could more than offset numbers or advanced equipment. During the Winter War of 1939 to 1940 and the Continuation of War of 1941 to 1944, Finnish pilots destroyed 1,808 Russian aircraft in aerial combat and achieved an overall kill ratio of 7.5:1, while never operating more than 150 fighters at any one time. A large proportion of these Finnish victories were chalked up by Brewster's portly fighter.

With 94.17 victories—thirty-four in Buffaloes—Eino I. Juutilainen of LeVv 24 emerged as Finland's highest-scoring World War II ace. During 437 combat missions, Juutilainen shot down no fewer than twenty-two different types of Soviet-, British-, and American-built aircraft flown by Russian pilots, yet his own aircraft was never holed by enemy fire. His achievements brought him awards of the Mannerheim Cross not once but twice, making him one of only two Finnish flyers to be so decorated.

Eagles' Prey

Carroll W. "Red" McColpin, RAF

Roy Grinnell

CARROLL W. "RED" MCCOLPIN WAS ONE OF THOSE AMERICANS WHO WAS so passionate in his hatred of Nazi evil, and so convinced of the rightness of democracy and the inevitability of war with Hitler that he took action even before his country did. Born in Buffalo, New York, in 1914, he taught himself to fly, and when war erupted in Europe, he headed north and enlisted in the RAF in Canada. Upon finishing pilot training, he first went to No. 607 Squadron, then to No. 121 Squadron, and finally to No. 71 "Eagle" Squadron, based at RAF Station North Weald.

In the fall of 1941, No. 71 Squadron was flying Spitfire Vbs in the air defense of Great Britain, a task that usually amounted to baiting the Luftwaffe's Bf 109Fs and Fw 190As up to fight. Such was the case on 2 October, 1941, when P/O McColpin in Spitfire Mk Vb AB908 coded XR-Y was flying as wingman to Squadron Leader Stanley Meares. When eighteen to twenty Messerschmitts from the crack III./JG 2 *Richthofen* were sighted a few hundred feet below, McColpin called out the bogeys to Meares, then both dived to the attack. Firing a one-half-second burst from under fifty yards (45m), the American saw his victim burst into flames and spiral down, then he rolled off to attack a second Messerschmitt. The second 109 also pulled up, then dived trailing smoke and apparently hit the ground. McColpin was duly credited with two Bf 109Es destroyed, but air combat is fast and deceptive—German records for 2 October show three Bf 109Fs from III./JG 2 making belly landings with severe damage after air combat. No German pilots were reported casualties that day.

Before the war's end, McColpin was credited with six more German aircraft shot down. After the war he remained in the USAF, where he went on to command the 31st Fighter Group and later the Fourth Air Force. He retired as a major general in 1968.

Desert Victory

Gerhard Homuth, Luftwaffe

Nicolas Trudgian

GERHARD HOMUTH HAD BEEN, LIKE MANY HIGHLY SUCCESSFUL LUFTWAFFE officers, a professional soldier since the mid-1930s. He had initially enlisted in the *Kriegsmarine* but transferred to the Luftwaffe in 1937, where he later flew in the service's aerobatics unit as a member of 2.(*Jagd*)/LG 2. By 1939 he was the *Gruppen Adjutant* for I./JG 27 *Afrika*. On 1 February, 1940, Homuth was given command of 3./JG 27, a *Staffel* that he was to lead with great distinction under primitive conditions in North Africa during 1941 and early 1942. He was awarded the coveted *Ritterkreuz* on 16 June, 1941, after his 22nd victory; by 9 February, 1942, his score had risen to forty. Beyond any question, Homuth's most notable protégé and pilot in North Africa was Hans-Joachim Marseille, a *Wunderkind* who by March 1942 had already exceeded his *Staffelkapitän's* score and would go on to achieve 158 air victories (see *Hunters in the Desert*, p. 56).

On 8 June, 1942, Homuth was promoted to command I./JG 27, and a month and a day later, he shot down his 50th victim. By the time I./JG 27 left North Africa at the end of October, he had raised his score to 60. Very soon after the unit's withdrawal to Europe, however, Homuth fell seriously ill and carried out only administrative duties until the end of July 1943. At that time he was given command of I./JG 54 *Grünherz* on the northern Russian front. His long absence from combat and/or the very different conditions on the Eastern Front may have been Homuth's undoing, however, for on 2 August, 1943, after only five days at the helm of I./JG 54, his Fw 190A-6 was shot down after a twenty-minute battle with Russian fighters, and he was thenceforth listed as missing. By this point he had completed about 450 combat sorties and had sixty-three aerial victories to his credit—fifteen in the West; forty-six in Africa; and two in the East.

First Blood

David L. "Tex" Hill, AVG

Roy Grinnell

THREE DAYS INTO THE NEW YEAR OF 1942, THE JAPANESE AGAIN TOOK to the skies in Burma, maintaining the intensive campaign against the AVG and RAF they had begun weeks before. On this day, nine Nakajima Ki 27 Nates from Capt. Yoyoki Eto's 77th *Sentai* took off from Raheng, fifty miles (80km) inside Thailand, and made a strafing attack on Moulmein Airfield in Burma, home to some obsolete Westland Wapitis and Hawker Audaxes of No. 4 Coastal Defense Flight, Indian Air Force. While the Moulmein raid was underway, Flying Tiger Sqdn. Ldr. John "Scarsdale Jack" Newkirk led three P-40s from his 2nd Pursuit Squadron ("Panda Bears") on a retaliatory strike against Raheng, the very base to which the Nates were now returning.

The first three of the Japanese fighters had just touched down when Newkirk, Vice-Sqdn. Ldr. James Howard, and Flt. Ldr. David L. "Tex" Hill pounced on them at 250 mph (400kph) out of the sun. In the ensuing melee, Newkirk picked a Nate off Howard's tail but in turn had to be rescued by Hill, who blasted a Ki 27 that had turned in behind his squadron commander. Newkirk then claimed another Nate, while Howard shot up several on the ground. Having exhausted their surprise, the Flying Tigers broke off the attack; all returned safely to Mingladon, where the usual reenactment, back-slapping, and rude horseplay ensued. Newkirk initially denied that Hill had had to pull his fat out of the fire, but an inspection revealed eleven bullet holes in the tail of his P-40C, while Hill's own no. 48 had collected thirty-three hits in the wing. Hill had saved his squadron leader, but his first blood had come very close to being his last.

LIEUTENANT (JUNIOR GRADE) IRA "IKE" KEPFORD

Ike Kepford, a member of Lieutenant Commander Blackburn's Fighting Squadron 17, downed sixteen Japanese planes during the war. On 5 November, 1943, Kepford shot down three dive bombers and one torpedo bomber to help frustrate a Japanese attack on the fast carrier *Essex*, while its planes were returning from an attack on Rabaul, New Britain.

Ace in a Day

Vern E. Graham, USN

Stan Stokes

VERN EARL GRAHAM WON A RARE PLACE FOR HIMSELF IN THE ELITE community of aces when, on 12 June, 1943, he shot down five Japanese Zeroes on one mission in the defense of Guadalcanal. Born on 13 September, 1919, in Rocky Ford, Colorado, Graham had joined the U.S. Navy in June 1941 and had become an aviation cadet. Soon after his commissioning as an ensign on 3 April, 1942, he joined VF-11 (the "Sundowners") and went with it to Guadalcanal in the southwest Pacific.

During an operation over the Solomons on 12 June, 1943, a large number of Japanese fighters jumped a formation of Marine F4U Corsairs, but were in turn bounced by VF-11's Wildcats. In the ensuing action, Graham shot down five Zeroes about ten miles (16km) northwest of the Russell Islands, thus becoming an ace in a day, indeed, an ace in one mission. Yet more remarkably, his fighter was an obsolescent, outclassed Grumman F4F-4 Wildcat with BuAir no. 12119, normally an odds-off match for the Zero. Unfortunately, the fight had cost the young naval aviator the last of his fuel, and he cracked up his aircraft while attempting a landing in the Russell Islands. Seriously injured, Graham claimed no more enemy aircraft and finished his Navy tour with the five victories he had racked up in one amazing day.

Roy Grinnell

First Marine Ace

Marion E. Carl, USMC

Roy Grinnell

CAPT. MARION E. CARL WAS AMONG THE EARLY NAVY AND MARINE CORPS flyers who struggled through the dark, daunting, discouraging days of 1942 to hold, then turn back, Japan's march across the Pacific. It was a time when a few had to do much with very little.

After graduating from Oregon State University in 1938 with a B.S. in aeronautical engineering, Carl entered the Army but quickly transferred to the Marine Corps, winning his golden wings late in 1939. The day after Pearl Harbor, his fighter squadron—VMF-221 "Fighting Falcons"—was loaded aboard the USS *Saratoga* and shipped off to defend Midway, a tiny but strategically vital speck in the mid-Pacific. VMF-221 arrived on Christmas Day, 1941, to find that the island's defenses were pitifully weak. This situation improved little over the next five months.

On 3 June, 1942, the Japanese struck Midway full force. On his first combat mission the next day, Carl shot down a Zero and damaged two others, an action that earned him the prestigious Navy Cross for valor. Following the stunning Japanese defeat at Midway, Carl transferred to VMF-223, which arrived on Guadalcanal on 20 August. Air action was immediate and relentless, and within thirty-five days, he had claimed five more Zeros and 7.5 bombers, making him the first ace in Marine Corps history. The years 1943–45 brought a second Navy Cross, command of VMF-223, promotion to the rank of major, and a final score of 18.5 aerial victories.

Carl's postwar career was spectacular and packed with accomplishments. He became a helicopter pilot, tested early jets, set speed records in the Douglas Skystreak, served in Vietnam, commanded the 2nd Marine Air Wing, and finally retired with the rank of major general in 1973. It was a peaceful retirement until June 1997, when the general was murdered at age eighty-two in a robbery of his Roseburg, Oregon, home.

Hunters in the Desert

Hans-Joachim Marseille, Luftwaffe

Robert Taylor

IN HISTORY'S TINY COMMUNITY OF ALL-TIME GREATEST FIGHTER PILOTS, Hans-Joachim Marseille enjoys his own very special place. He established himself as the Luftwaffe's highest scoring pilot in the Mediterranean theater of operations by destroying 158 RAF aircraft on the Channel front and in North Africa. Although the majority of his victories with 3./JG 27 in North Africa were over technologically inferior aircraft such as Hurricanes and Curtiss P-40s, the RAF pilots were well trained and often enjoyed numerical superiority. Foes and odds aside, there can be no doubt Marseille possessed an inborn talent for air-to-air gunnery that was matched by only a handful of pilots, Axis or Allied. His snap deflection shooting in dogfights against more maneuverable foes became the stuff of awed legend. His destruction of six Curtiss P-40s in eleven minutes with the expenditure of ten rounds of 20mm and 180 rounds of 7.92mm ammunition—a feat verified by his wingman and ground crew—remains one of the most extraordinary incidents ever recorded in the history of aerial combat. So too does his destruction of seventeen RAF fighters during one day, a one-day claim exceeded only by Emil Lang on the Eastern Front. Given such a remarkable record, there is a certain irony in his death by in-flight mechanical failure. One can only speculate what this remarkable young flyer—he was twenty-three at the time—might have accomplished had he lived beyond September 1942. Regardless, Marseille became, and remains, a giant within the select company of the Luftwaffe's *Ritterkreuzträger*.

After the Battle

No. 611 "West Lancashire" Squadron, RAF

Robert Taylor

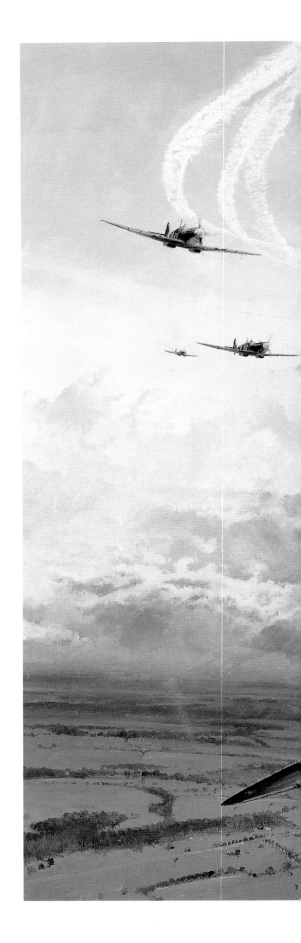

DURING THE 1930S, THE ROYAL AIR FORCE FORMED A NUMBER OF so-called Auxiliary Air Force squadrons—reserve units somewhat similar to U.S. Air National Guard squadrons—raised within a given locality and often more or less snootily regarded by RAF regulars as a dilettante militia. This disdain was compounded by the obsolescent bomber equipment of most AAF units. The exigencies of 1939 and 1940, however, saw many Auxiliary Air Force squadrons converted to fighters and thrown into first-line operations, where, with some experience, they proved every bit as effective as their regular service cousins.

No. 611 "West Lancashire" Squadron was typical of the Auxiliary Air Force squadron swept into the cauldron of full-scale war in 1939. It was initially formed of volunteers from Lancashire in northwest England (mostly Liverpool men) and equipped with Hawker Hind light bombers. The unit's arms combined the red rose of the House of Lancaster with a trident from the armorial bearings of the City of Liverpool. Its motto was "Beware! Beware!"

No. 611 became a fighter squadron with Spitfire Mk. Is in 1939. Based at RAF Station Duxford and then at Tern Hill during 1939 and 1940, elements of the squadron were detached to RAF Station Martlesham Heath in June 1940 to cover the Dunkirk evacuation. As part of 12 Group at Tern Hill and Digby the unit played a limited role in the Battle of Britain, but during 1941 it flew extensive Rodeos and Circuses over the Channel as part of the so-called Nonstop Offensive. Between July 1942 and July 1943 No. 611 took its Spitfire Mk IXs on similar fighter sweeps over northern France, and it is this operational era that Robert Taylor has portrayed in *After the Battle*. No. 611 Squadron operated several Spitfire Mk IXs in the serial range BS1—, thus, FY-K cannot be more precisely identified.

The Unlucky Eight

James E. Swett, USMC

Stan Stokes

JIM SWETT WAS BORN IN SEATTLE, WASHINGTON, IN 1920 AND RECEIVED the golden wings of a Marine Corps aviator in April 1942. Assigned to VMF-221 "Fighting Falcons," he arrived on Guadalcanal with his squadron on 16 March, 1943. Swett's baptism of fire came just three weeks later, in the mid-afternoon of 7 April, when a huge formation of Aichi D3A1 Vals with fighter escort appeared over Tulagi Island, twenty-two miles north (35km) of American airfields on Guadalcanal. The Marines' F4F-4 Wildcats cut through the spatted Japanese dive bombers like death's scythe; Swett shot down three in quick succession before being hit by friendly anti-aircraft fire. In his now-damaged aircraft, the Marine continued to attack the Vals and downed four more, with an eighth possibly downed but officially credited only as a probable. This eighth Val may have been unlucky in another sense, too, for its gunner shot down Swett's Wildcat (BuAir No. 12036). Wounded, Swett ditched into the waters of "the Slot" between Tulagi and Guadalcanal but was soon fished out. For this action, Swett was awarded the Medal of Honor by the Commanding General of Marine Aviation in the South Pacific, Maj. Gen. Ralph J. Mitchell, on 9 October, 1943.

After three combat tours with VMF-221 on Guadalcanal and Vella Lavella and one on the USS *Bunker Hill* in 1945, Swett finished the war with 15.5 aerial victories and 4 probables. He left active duty in 1945, enjoyed a postwar career manufacturing marine pumps and turbines, and retired from the Marine Corps Reserve with the rank of Colonel in 1970.

Warm Reception

Joseph J. "Joe" Foss, USMC

James Dietz

Medal of Honor–winner Capt. Joe Foss was the first U.S. pilot to tie the record of Eddie Rickenbacker, the leading American ace of World War I, with twenty-six victories.

MOST AVIATION ARTISTS ARE INCLINED TO PORTRAY THEIR subjects in their natural element, usually choosing those fleeting dramatic moments of history that combat represents. With *Warm Reception*, however, James Dietz has taken the unusual and appealing approach of portraying Marine ace Capt. Joseph Jacob "Joe" Foss of VMF-121 in his Grumman F4F-4 on the ground after a mission at Henderson Field, Guadalcanal. The resulting image not only honors a notable Marine Corps ace but sensitively captures the primitive tropical environment of Henderson Field, Guadalcanal, as well as the camaraderie and team spirit involved in every great fighting unit.

Foss, a native of Sioux Falls, South Dakota, joined the Marine Corps on the eve of World War II and was designated a Marine aviator on 29 March, 1941. Initially a flight instructor at Pensacola, he was promoted to captain in mid-1942 and arrived with VMF-121 on Guadalcanal on 9 October. Before the end of the year, he had shot down an amazing twenty-three Japanese aircraft, mostly fighters, and added another three in January 1943. His score of twenty-six made Foss the all-time leading Marine fighter ace.

On 18 May, 1943, President Roosevelt decorated Foss with the United States' highest military award, the Medal of Honor. This was, however, merely the first in a string of life achievements. In 1946, Foss resigned from the Marine Corps Reserve to become a lieutenant colonel in the South Dakota National Guard. He subsequently rose to the rank of brigadier general, entered the state legislature, and was elected governor of South Dakota in 1954 and again in 1956. Between 1959 and 1966 he served as commissioner of the American Football League and between 1972 and 1978 as director of public affairs for KLM Royal Dutch Airlines. He was president of the National Rifle Association from 1988 to 1990 and remains active in the adult ministry of the Campus Crusade for Christ International.

Zero Fighter Sweep

Kenneth A. Walsh, USMC

Roy Grinnell

THE AIR RAID ALARM WAILED ON GUADALCANAL AT 1132 ON 13 MAY, 1943, as it had almost daily for the past eight months. Island radars had picked up an incoming formation of bogeys approaching from the northwest—Japanese aircraft apparently coming down "the Slot" between Guadalcanal and the Florida Islands just as they usually did. The American reaction was to scramble off the twelve F4U-1 Corsairs of VMF-124 "Checkerboards." Easing open the throttle of his Corsair's Pratt & Whitney R-2800-8, twenty-six-year-old 1st Lt. Ken Walsh was airborne first and was vectored north with his flight toward the Florida Islands. Reaching the intercept point, however, Walsh's flight discovered the bogeys were inbound USAAF P-38s. As the four Marine fighters turned away, Walsh heard Guadalcanal ground control vector his squadron commander, Maj. William E. Gise, with eight Corsairs northwest toward the Russell Islands at "Angels 20." Walsh radioed Gise that his flight would join him, turned west, and climbed toward twenty-five thousand feet (7,500m). Within minutes, a raging air battle was in sight fifteen miles (24km) east of the Russell Islands. Peeling off from a right echelon, Walsh led his flight headlong into the melee. Selecting an A6M5 Zero to his far left, he pulled his big bent-wing fighter around, met the Zero nearly head on, and opened fire. Seconds later, the Japanese fighter broke off, trailing smoke and mortally wounded. Within minutes, Walsh had scored twice more and damaged a fourth Zero. He had become VMF-124's first ace and the first ace in the Corsair.

On 8 February, 1944, President Roosevelt hung the Medal of Honor around Walsh's neck in a White House ceremony. Walsh subsequently returned to the Pacific theater, claimed one additional Zero, and finished the war with a final score of twenty-one aerial victories, making him the fourth-ranked World War II Marine aviator.

Not My Turn to Die

Robert S. Johnson, USAAF

Jim Laurier

Robert S. Johnson's harrowing experience is a testament not only to the high-scoring ace's personal grit, but also to the tough skin of the Thunderbolt fighter, which, despite severe damage at the hands of a German fighter, simply refused to die.

AERIAL COMBAT IS A STRANGE, SOMETIMES SURREAL, EXPERIENCE, IN WHICH the unexplained and the unexplainable recur with surprising frequency. Lt. Robert S. Johnson's encounter with a Fw 190 on 16 June, 1943, was an such event; it could have come straight out of *Ripley's Believe It or Not*.

On 26 June, 1943, P-47C Thunderbolts from the 56th Fighter Group's 61st, 62nd, and 63rd Fighter Squadrons ("Zemke's Wolfpack") were launched from AAF Station Boxted to escort an Eighth AF operation against Villacoublay, France. The mission was going smoothly—until the American formation was bounced by Fw 190s from JG 2 and JG 26, which proceeded to shoot down five Thunderbolts and damage seven others, two beyond repair.

One of the damaged P-47s, the P-47C-2-RE s/n 41-6235 (HV-P, *Half Pint*) belonged to 61st Fighter Squadron pilot Lt. Robert S. Johnson, who had won his first victory in the same airplane on 13 June. On the 26th it was a different matter. As Johnson later related in his autobiography, *Thunderbolt!*, a Fw 190 caught him in its sights and riddled his airplane with machine gun bullets and 20mm cannon shells. One 20mm round exploded in the cockpit, another passed through the rear part of the sliding hood, jamming it closed. Wounded and half-blind, Johnson could not bail out and had to limp home to survive. Any other fighter would probably have gone down, but the Thunderbolt was one tough customer, and now it showed. *Half Pint's* engine kept running, there was no fire, and things looked hopeful until another Fw 190 latched onto the crippled American. The German mercilessly hammered the helpless Thunderbolt, exhausting his machine gun ammunition without result. According to Johnson, the astonished and no doubt bewildered German pilot then eased alongside, studied his would-be victim, saluted, and turned away, leaving the shaken American to nurse his flying sieve back to Boxted. Lt. Johnson landed safely, returned to operations within a few weeks, and went on to finish the war with twenty-eight victories. *Half Pint* never flew again.

Mission Accomplished!

Rex Barber, USAAF

Roy Grinnell

The controversy over exactly who shot down the plane carrying Japanese Admiral Isoroku Yamamoto (above) in April 1943 has never been entirely resolved. Two pilots—Rex Barber and Thomas Lamphier—vied for sole credit for the victory.

THE DOWNING OF JAPANESE ADMIRAL ISOROKU YAMAMOTO on Easter Sunday, 18 April, 1943, was unquestionably the single most stellar fighter action of World War II—an amazing coup that doubtlessly changed the course of the conflict. The mission per se was astonishing enough, but its fame has been amplified even further by a raging controversy over who actually shot down the admiral.

The end for Yamamoto began on 14 April, 1943, when the U.S. Navy decoded a radio message detailing his impending visit by air to Bougainville, 360 miles (579km) from Guadalcanal. The commander-in-chief of the Imperial Japanese Navy, it appeared, was going to inspect his men on the 18th of that month. The intercept was an incredible "snag," and U.S. command authorities jumped on the opportunity to get Yamamoto. But how to do it? USAAF fighters would have to make a split-second visual interception at a great distance over water while approaching in total secrecy, including radio silence. Their schedules—and Yamamoto's—would have to match perfectly.

Maj. John Mitchell, commander of the 339th Fighter Squadron on Guadalcanal, was handed the Yamamoto mission. He plotted a 481-mile (770km) outbound flight path that skirted Japanese defenses, a reach made possible only by newly arrived 310-gallon (1,180l) drop tanks for his unit's P-38 Lightnings. At 0710 on 18 April, Mitchell led his eighteen-plane force off airstrip Fighter Two; about two and three-quarter hours later—right on time—the formation sighted the two Mitsubishi G4M Betty bombers carrying Yamamoto and his staff over the southwestern tip of Bougainville. Both Bettys were shot down, with official credit for the one carrying Yamamoto going to Capt. Thomas Lamphier and 1st Lt. Rex T. Barber. Subsequently, however, a running squabble developed over which pilot actually "got Yamamoto." An official Air Force review in 1991 affirmed the shared credit, but many independent authorities believe that credit should go exclusively to Rex Barber.

Fighter Two—Guadalcanal

Guadalcanal 1943, USAAF

Jim Laurier

IN THE ALLIES' ISLAND-HOPPING STRATEGY TO RETAKE THE PACIFIC, BASES for air power always loomed large—in many ways, the Pacific war was driven by the need to secure fixed, unsinkable "aircraft carriers" that could protect existing supply lines or cover the next big leap. So it was with Guadalcanal. Soon after the American landings on the island in August 1942, American combat engineers, working under fire, turned it into a usable "aircraft carrier." Henderson Field, begun by the Japanese, was completed, and Fighter One and Fighter Two were carved out of the lush, malaria-ridden jungle.

Overshadowed by Henderson Field, Fighter Two is the least known of the Guadalcanal airfields; today it can scarcely be found on any campaign map except those in the Army Air Force's official history. Completed at the beginning of 1943, the strip was nothing more than a thirty-two-hundred-foot (960m) runway surfaced with crushed coral and nestled within dense palm groves a few hundred yards from the waters of "the Slot" on Guadalcanal's northern coast. While Henderson Field was home to the large Marine air presence on the island, Fighter Two hosted a modest number of USAAF fighter units that came and went irregularly. Those known to have been at Fighter Two in 1943 include the 339th Fighter Squadron, the 12th Fighter Squadron, and the 68th Fighter Squadron. Despite its obscurity and simplicity, however, Fighter Two deserves an enduring place in history, since it was from here that the 339th Fighter Squadron launched the 18 P-38s that intercepted and shot down Admiral Isoroku Yamamoto on 18 April, 1943.

With *Fighter Two*, Jim Laurier has captured a typical moment in USAAF operations on Guadalcanal as a P-38 lifts off, possibly to "get Yamamoto." The plane is coated with stirred-up coral dust and has been fueled and serviced under the most primitive conditions imaginable.

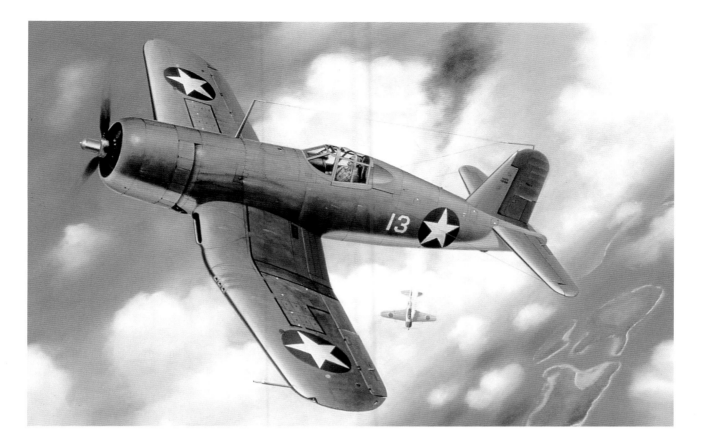

Dogfight Over the Russells

Kenneth A. Walsh, USMC

Mike Machat

THE INTRODUCTION OF THE CHANCE-VOUGHT F4U-1 CORSAIR INTO U.S. Navy and Marine Corps squadrons early in 1943 was a tangible sign of the shift in the tide of battle in the Pacific, for these were the fighters that signaled the demise of the once-fearsome Zero. Big and burly, powerful and hard-hitting, the Corsair and its companion, the Grumman F6F Hellcat, quickly replaced the Grumman Wildcat as the Navy's and Marine Corps' aerial weapons of choice to defeat Japan. Both the Corsair and the Hellcat were intended as carrier fighters, but many Corsair squadrons, especially those of the Marines, operated from island bases such as Henderson Field on Guadalcanal. Both the Corsair and Hellcat could take on any Japanese fighter on equal or better terms, but the Corsair also came to have a significant role as a ground attack machine, firing rockets and pitching bombs into enemy positions with deadly accuracy. Overall, the F4U was one of the Navy's principal

instruments of victory, and so effective that it soldiered on throughout the Korean conflict, wreaking havoc on North Korean and Chinese forces just as it had on the Japanese.

Lt. Kenneth A. Walsh was one of the first Corsair pilots to prove that the bent-wing bird from Chance-Vought was a winner. On 1 April, 1943, about six weeks after landing on Guadalcanal, Walsh and seven other Corsair pilots from Maj. William E. Gise's VMF-124 tangled with a much superior force of Japanese fighters over the Russell Islands, thirty miles (50km) northwest of Guadalcanal. The Marine flyers broke up the Japanese formation; Walsh alone claimed two Zeroes and an Aichi D3A Val dive bomber. Six weeks later, on 13 May, Walsh became an ace, and by the end of the war he was an ace four times over. He remained in the Marine Corps after the war, flew in Korea, and retired as a lieutenant colonel in 1962.

Day of the Fighters

I. *Gruppe* JG 1 *Oesau*, Luftwaffe

Nicolas Trudgian

NICOLAS TRUDGIAN'S DRAMATIC *DAY OF THE FIGHTERS* DEPICTS FIVE
Fw 190As of 1./JG 1 *Oesau* returning low over the Dutch countryside to their
base at Deelen, The Netherlands, on 17 August, 1943. The Focke Wulfs have
just done battle with several hundred Eighth AF B-17s attacking the ball-
bearing works at Schweinfurt and the Messerschmitt factory at Regensburg,
Germany. This historic operation was one of the USAAF's first large-scale deep
penetrations of German air space, and it was very costly, since at this time
Allied fighters could escort bombers only part of the way into the continent.
The USAAF 1st and 4th Bombardment Wings had dispatched 376 aircraft,
sixty of which (16 percent) never returned. The Luftwaffe had put up most of
its fighter units in the West, and about forty-seven of the bombers were lost to
single-engine fighter attack. On the other hand, the Luftwaffe lost forty-two fighters to Allied fire. The I./JG 1 claimed four B-17s shot down and nine driven out
of their formation while losing three of its fighters and damaging four others.

The Focke Wulfs in *Day of the Fighters* all sport I./JG 1's checkered cowlings,
a motif unique to this *Gruppe* during much of 1943. The lead aircraft "white 4"
from 1./JG 1 is very probably Fw 190A-4 *WNr.* 14 0601 built by Focke Wulf
at Marienburg about July 1942 and probably delivered new to 1./JG 1. On 9
September—about a month after reaching the unit—it ran off the runway at
Schipol Airport, Amsterdam, during a noncombat flight and collapsed a main
landing gear leg (10 percent damage). Returned to service with 1./JG 1, the
WNr. 14 0601 was involved in a taxiing accident at Schiphol during a noncombat flight on 25 June 1943 and suffered 15 percent damage. The aircraft
is last mentioned in surviving records on 13 November, 1943, when it was
belly-landed by an unknown I./JG 1 pilot near Bielefeld, Germany, after air
combat and seriously damaged (45 percent). Unfortunately, none of the names
of the pilots who flew the "white 4" are known today.

MAJOR ERICH HARTMANN

The highest-scoring ace of all time, Erich Hartmann started in aviation as a member of a German civilian glider club while a teenager in the 1930s. Gliding, he later said, sharpened his instincts so that he could sense structural or aerodynamic problems before they became critical. Hartmann received credit for 352 victories, eleven during two sorties on the same day, but had to crash-land or take to his parachute sixteen times. When Germany collapsed, he chose to surrender to the Americans, who turned him over to the Soviets, against whom he had scored most of his kills. He spent ten years as a prisoner, joined West Germany's new Luftwaffe upon being repatriated, and became the organization's commander.

Russian Roulette

Russian Yak-9s Over Kursk, 1943

Robert Taylor

ROBERT TAYLOR'S *RUSSIAN ROULETTE* RECAPTURES A TYPICAL dogfight on the central part of the Eastern Front in mid-1943. A single Bf 109G-6 is tangling with several Yak-9Ds of the Soviet VVS, the Bf 109 skidding around in a maximum-G bank that leaves contrails streaming from the Messerschmitt's wingtips.

Several details in Taylor's painting are worth noting. By the time of the Battle of Kursk in mid-1943, Soviet equipment and pilots had improved dramatically over their performance of 1941. The Yak-9D was a superb dogfighting machine—light, agile, and sufficiently fast, it matched the Bf 109G-6 in speed and could exceed it in most combat maneuvres. Given conditions on the Eastern Front and Soviet doctrine, its lack of range, electronic equipment, and simple "throw-away" construction in no way impaired its effectiveness. By mid-1943, too, Soviet pilot training and experience equalled that of the average German pilot, and Russian morale and esprit de corps had made much progress from the grim days of 1941–1942.

The outcome of *Russian Roulette*, however, is by no means certain. The markings on the Bf 109 point to a crack pilot from the *Stab* of JG 52 or one of the wing's *Gruppenstäbe*, possibly a one-hundred-victory ace such as *Oberstltn.* Dietrich Hrabak. Being outnumbered four-to-one hardly intimidated such men, who had been routinely beating equal or greater odds and running up huge scores since the invasion of Russia in June 1941. The outcome of *Russian Roulette*, therefore, will depend, as it so often did, not so much on airplanes as on pure nerve, skill, and the luck of the draw.

Maj. Gen. Dietrich Hraback was shot down on the first day of the war, but went on to score 125 air-to-air victories for the Luftwaffe. He was awarded the Knights Cross with Oak Leaves.

High Tide of Summer

Gunther Rall, Luftwaffe

Jim Laurier

JIM LAURIER'S *HIGH TIDE OF SUMMER* PERFECTLY CAPTURES THE Luftwaffe's paradoxical situation on the Eastern Front in late summer 1942: it was an air force winning almost all the battles but about to lose the war. During 1941 and early 1942, Luftwaffe fighter wings such as JG 52, JG 54, JG 3, JG 77, and JG 51 had run wild against the Soviet Air Force; dozens of pilots in these units had run up scores of 50 or more against ill-trained, doctrinally-bound, and poorly-equipped Russian opponents. Not without reason had the Eastern Front become known within the Luftwaffe as *Jagdflieger Paradies*—"Fighter Pilot's Paradise." But this situation was about to change radically—by August 1942, the German Air Force had reached its high tide, and the currents would soon turn against it. Stalingrad began in November 1942, and from this time on the Luftwaffe was forced into a defensive retreat that led only one way.

Several German fighter wings shared the halcyon early days on the Eastern Front, but none ran up higher scores there than JG 52. Deployed in the Ukraine and southern Russia from June 1941 onwards, JG 52 eventually produced the three highest scoring aces of all time, Erich Hartmann (352 victories), Gerhard Barkhorn (301), and Günther Rall (275). Of these three, Rall had been first off the mark. By 28 November 1941 he had thirty-six air victories, but on that date a Russian fighter shot him down, and the ensuing crash landing kept him from flying again until late summer of 1942. By this time, Rall had fallen well behind his contemporaries, a number of whom had exceeded one hundred victories and already had won their *Ritterkreuze*.

The *High Tide of Summer* depicts a Bf 109G-2 of 8./JG 52 flown by Rall during the late summer and early fall of 1942, a time when he had just returned to combat and was playing catch up with with his rampaging comrades. Around the Messerschmitts the Russian steppes stretch silently and endlessly to the horizon, impassively waiting to swallow up the German intruders just as they had swallowed Napoleon's invasion 130 years before.

Gunther Rall closed out the war as the second highest scoring Ace of all time, with 275 aerial victories, and was awarded the Knights Cross with Oak leaves and Swords. After the war, he became part of the Budesluftwaffe (the new Luftwaffe), and even spent time training on new planes in the United States in the 1950s.

Gunfight Over Rabaul

VMF-214 "Black Sheep," USMC

Nicolas Trudgian

The Black Sheep squadron, pictured surrounding Commander Gregory "Pappy" Boyington in a preflight meeting, produced nine aces, and tallied an impressive 126 official aerial victories.

THE VMF-214 SERVED ITS FIRST TOUR OF DUTY IN THE SOUTHWEST Pacific between February 1943 and September 1943, flying from island bases on Espiritu Santu and Guadalcanal. It then underwent a second southwest Pacific deployment to Munda during September and October and to Vella Lavella from November 1943 to January 1944, after which it returned to the United States. Throughout 1943, VMF-214 flew the Chance-Vought F4U-1 and -1A Corsair, which it used with great success against improved Mitsubishi A6M5 Zero fighters over Rabaul, the gateway to New Britain and New Guinea. It was during this second tour in the Southwest Pacific that the unit became known as the "Black Sheep" after its flamboyant and unconventional commander, Maj. Gregory "Pappy" Boyington. In a third and final deployment VMF-214 was sent aboard the USS *Franklin* in February 1945, and it was operating from the carrier when the ship was badly damaged and knocked out of action by kamikazes on 19 March. The squadron finished the war with a total of 126 aerial victories and thirty-four probables.

True combat performance aside, the "Black Sheep" have gotten much attention in the postwar media; indeed, after the Flying Tigers, the squadron may be the best known U.S. air unit of World War II. Some of this reporting is more or less accurate, but much is sheer Hollywood, and it is now difficult to disentangle fact from fiction in the popular mind. Squadron leader Gregory Boyington's autobiography, *Baa Baa Black Sheep* (1958), helped launch the unit's legend, but it was really Robert Conrad's semi-fictional weekly television series of 1976–78 that forever established the "Black Sheep" in U.S. military folklore.

Black Sheep Over Rabaul

Gregory "Pappy" Boyington, USMC

Stan Stokes

VMF-214's MOST COLORFUL PERSONALITY DURING 1943 WAS WITHOUT doubt its commanding officer, Maj. Gregory "Pappy" Boyington, an aggressive and distinctive Marine who had his own way of approaching life in uniform. In the mid-1930s Boyington became a naval aviator, and on 1 July, 1937, he was commissioned as a lieutenant in the Marine Corps. He flew with the AVG during early 1942 and asserted he had six victories, though he was paid for only 3½. Disgusted, Boyington left the AVG, returned to the United States, and was eventually dishonorably discharged from the Flying Tigers. He rejoined the Marines, was commissioned as a first lieutenant on 29 September, 1942, and was promoted to major in November 1942. In April 1943, Boyington was given command of VMF-122, though he lost the post in early June after breaking a leg in a drunken barracks contretemps.

Finally, on 7 September, 1943, he was assigned to lead the reconstituted VMF-214 on its second tour in the southwest Pacific, a unit which not surprisingly became known as the "Black Sheep." Boyington commanded the squadron until 3 January, 1944, when he was shot down in F4U-1A BuAir no. 17915 and became a POW. While a Japanese prisoner, Boyington received the Medal of Honor for one action over Kahili Airfield on 17 October, 1943; the award went in absentia to his mother, and President Truman was not able to decorate him in person until October 1945. Official records credit Boyington with twenty-two Marine victories, and six with the AVG, for a total of twenty-eight.

Boyington remained in the Marine Corps for a short time after the war, but retired as a lieutenant colonel in 1947. Much of the remainder of his life was a struggle with alcoholism; he died of cancer in Fresno, California, on 11 January, 1988.

Legendary Black Sheep leader Gregory "Pappy" Boyington was one of the top Marine aces of World War II. He was officially credited with twenty-eight aerial victories, though some sources suspect his score was closer to twenty-four.

Salute to the Jolly Rogers

VF-17 "Jolly Rogers," USN

Domenic DeNardo

IF THE SUCCESS OF FIGHTER UNITS WERE MEASURED ONLY IN TERMS OF aerial victories, then VF-17 "Jolly Rogers" goes to the head of the list of U.S. Navy squadrons active during World War II. During tours of duty on New Georgia and Bougainville in late 1943, it was officially credited with 152.50 aerial victories, to which a further 161 were added during a 1944 deployment on board the USS *Hornet*. The squadron's successes were divided among a number of aces—of which it produced at least twenty-four—as well as many pilots with fewer than five victories. VF-17's leading scorer was Ira C. Kepford, who ended the war with sixteen official aerial victories.

Members of VF-17 Squadron, the "Jolly Rogers," pose for a group photograph in front of the squadron scoreboard. One of the U.S. Navy's land-based units, and only the second to operate in-theater equipped with Corsair fighters, the Jolly Rogers scored an incredible 154 kills in just seventy-nine days during the Solomons Campaign.

COL. DONALD J.M. BLAKESLEE

Before the United States entered World War II, Donald J.M. Blakeslee joined the Royal Air Force. He served with 133 Squadron, one of the Eagle squadrons manned by American volunteers, and downed three German aircraft. He transferred to the U.S. Army Air Forces and scored 11.5 victories, most of them while flying the North American P-51. A respected tactician and leader, he served two tours as commander of the 4th Fighter Group in the United Kingdom, the highest-scoring group in the Eighth Air Force.

First Mustang Ace

Michael T. Russo, USAAF

Stan Stokes

THE IMMORTAL NORTH AMERICAN P-51 MUSTANG ORIGINATED AS A QUICK American response to British interest in something better than the Allison-engined Curtiss P-40. The airplane, it is said, was designed in New York hotel rooms in a month and went from paper to metal in 102 days. Incredibly, from the beginning it exhibited almost all "the right stuff." The first production Mustang—the RAF's Mustang Mk I—demonstrated superb speed and flight characteristics, but its Allison engine limited its altitude performance, and the brilliant airframe really did not come into its own until married to the magnificent Rolls-Royce Merlin engine in the fall of 1942. Meanwhile, the USAAF ordered five hundred P-51s for ground attack. It hung on bomb racks and dive brakes, redesignated the plane A-36A Apache, and relegated it to the dive bomber role. Early Mustangs, however, retained full dogfighting capability once their ordnance was released, and this potential was to help make Michael T. Russo the first Mustang ace.

Mike Russo was commissioned a second lieutenant in the Army Air Forces on 16 February, 1943, at Moore Field, Texas. He met the A-36A when he went to the Mediterranean theater of operations with the 16th Bombardment Squadron (Light) (later the 522nd Fighter-Bomber Squadron) in mid-1943. Operating from Sicilian and southern Italian bases, the 522nd FBS beat up Axis airfields, bridges, artillery positions, motor transport, shipping, and similar targets, and it supported the Salerno landings in September 1943. Russo claimed his first enemy plane, a Fw 190, near Salerno, Italy, on 13 September, and followed it with a Fi 167 biplane in October, a Ju 52 on 8 December, and two Bf 109s on 30 December, 1943, to become the first of many aces in the Mustang.

In Gallant Company

USMC Pilots, Solomon Islands, 1943

Robert Taylor

ROBERT TAYLOR'S IN GALLANT COMPANY DEPICTS U.S. MARINE CORPS Grumman F4F Wildcats and Chance-Vought F4U-1 Corsairs returning from a combat mission over the Solomon Islands sometime during 1943. As is usually the case with Taylor paintings, the rendering of the airplanes and the skyscape is remarkable, but in this case one immediately senses something deeper, something more profound: is this heaven, or perhaps an ascension to it? Then comes a blinding Dalí-esque metamorphosis from the real to the surreal, from a flight of planes to a figurative flight of militant angels in full glory. Taylor's brilliant rear lighting casts an ethereal aura around the lowest Wildcat, subtly drawing the viewer's attention to the plane without overtly advertising the reason. Ah, and then the epiphany unfolds. The aura is as much symbolic as compositional, for this Wildcat is slowly dying and will require all the support of its comrades—and perhaps divine intervention—to return home safely. Taylor's placement of the wounded Wildcat at the bottom front of a winglike "vee" further strengthens the impression of guardian angels as its pilot looks up to his squadron mates who hover close above, in gallant company . . .

The Forgotten Fighter

Aleksandr I. Pokryshkin and the Bell P-39 Aircobra

Stan Stokes

THE USAAF FIELDED FIVE MAJOR FIGHTER TYPES DURING WORLD WAR II; of these, the Bell P-39 Aircobra proved the least successful and achieved the least renown. Today it remains the geek of the United States' fighter family, an overly innovative, unconventional, and mostly unloved airplane that suffered from too little power and too many design faults to make the aviation hall of fame.

From an engineering standpoint, the Bell P-39 sprang from the breakneck technological progress, enormous conceptual flux, and tactical uncertainty that characterized military aviation at the end of the 1930s. At that time, the config-uration of future fighters was not at all clear, and the Bell Company placed its hopes for a USAAF contract on a radical design that combined a rear-mounted V-1710 Allison engine with a fearsome 37mm cannon, tricycle landing gear, and a cockpit entered through a car-type door. Unfortunately, this combination proved underpowered, "hot" during take-offs and landings, and unsettling to pilots. Needing fighters, the USAAF bought the P-39 anyway but soon discov-ered it could not hold its own under most combat conditions. What then were they to do with the thousands of Aircobras pouring off the lines?

During 1941 and 1942, some P-39s went to USAAF units in the southwest Pacific, where they were largely relegated to ground attack missions. The Soviet Union, however, was far and away the largest P-39 operator. Some 4,746 Aircobras reached the USSR through Lend-Lease, and one of these is depicted in Stan Stokes' *The Forgotten Fighter*. The pilot commemorated is Aleksandr I. Pokryshkin, the second-ranking Soviet ace and thrice-over "Hero of the Soviet Union" who is thought to have achieved forty-eight of his fifty-nine victories in a P-39 Aircobra. Pokryshkin served in combat from 1940 to 1945 and subse-quently pursued a military career, rising to air marshal and chairman of the Central Committee of DOSAAF before his death on 13 November, 1985.

DeNardo
97

Steadfast Against All Odds

368th Fighter Group, USAAF

Domenic DeNardo

BY THE SUMMER OF 1944, THE NINTH AF HAD BECOME A MASSIVE AERIAL sledgehammer made up of dozens of medium bomber and fighter-bomber groups that spent every good day making life miserable for the Wehrmacht. Most Ninth AF fighter-bomber groups operated the Thunderbolt, and the 368th FG was representative of these P-47 units, or *Jabos*, as the Germans called them. Throughout the days after 6 June, the 368th had ranged over northern France, tearing up fuel and ammunition depots, bridges, motor transport, trains, bridges, airfields, troop concentrations, and similar tactical targets wherever they could be found. For the most part, this was low down and dirty work involving bomb-laden approaches at eight to twelve thousand feet (2,400–3,600m), followed by fast dives on targets from out of the sun, the release of bombs, and a quick refor-mation and run for home. In good weather, this routine went on five or six times a day, day after day.

Normally, P-47 fighter-bombers did not go looking for German fighters, but the Luftwaffe hated the *Jabos*, and encounters with them were likely to be tooth-and-claw affairs. So it was in the forenoon of 14 June, 1944, when 2nd Lt. George Sutcliffe, flying D3-U as no. Two in *Whiskey Red* flight, was set on by forty-plus Bf 109s in the vicinity of Lisieux, France. The Bf 109s broke up the flight, and for the Americans it became a barroom brawl with every man for himself. After about five minutes of combat, Sutcliffe saw *Whiskey Red Four* go down; the pilot bailed out. According to his encounter report, Sutcliffe himself "had a running fight with twenty-plus Me 109s for about fifteen minutes, from the deck to 2,000 feet [600 m], until I got in the cloud layer and evaded them. During this time I received 20 MM hits in my left wing, fuselage, and tail." Sutcliffe came out of the cloud layer at two thousand feet [600 m] east of Le Havre, found *Whiskey Lead* and *Whiskey Three*, and headed home. A sweat-inducing, gut-wrenching episode for *Whiskey Red* flight, but all in a day's work for Ninth AF fighter-bombers—just one of the occupational hazards, one might say.

Unlucky Seven

David McCampbell, USN

Roy Grinnell

Cmdr. David McCampbell smiles from the cockpit of his F6F-3 Hellcat. The side panel boasts flags representing each of the thirty Japanese planes he'd shot down before this photo was taken; by the war's end, he'd added four more official victories.

MANY U.S. NAVY FLYERS RAN UP IMPRESSIVE SCORES DURING THE SO-CALLED Marianas Turkey Shoot of 19–20 June, 1944, but Cmdr. David McCampbell, commander of VF-15 and CVG-15 on USS *Essex*, was one of the most successful. Flying an F6F-3 Hellcat nicknamed *Mitzi*, McCampbell claimed five Yokosuka D4Y Judys destroyed and one probably destroyed over the sea 175 miles (280km) west-northwest of Guam at 1139. In a second mid-afternoon mission he sighted several Mitsubishi Zeroes attacking a Curtiss SOC seaplane that was trying to pick up a downed pilot off Orote Peninsula, Guam, and shot down two of them.

By the end of World War II, David McCampbell had official credit for thirty-four Japanese aircraft and five probables, making him the highest scoring U.S. Navy fighter pilot of all time. The U.S. Navy acknowledged his combat achievements and leadership with the Medal of Honor, the Navy Cross, a Legion of Merit, a Silver Star, three DFCs, and an Air Medal. McCampbell remained on active duty with the navy after the war and was promoted to captain in July 1952. He retired in July 1964 and died in Riviera Beach, Florida, on 30 June, 1996.

High Noon Over Alicante
Maj. Jay T. "Cock" Robbins, USAAC

Roy Grinnell

At war's end, Maj. Jay T. Robbins' twenty-two victories placed him in a tie with the 348th FG's Neel Kearby for fourth place among USAAF aces in the Pacific Theatre.

BY NOVEMBER 1944, MAJ. JAY ROBBINS HAD BEEN FLYING COMBAT missions in the South Pacific with the 80th Fighter Squadron of the 8th Fighter Group for two years. These had been years of success as a fighter pilot and as an officer in the most primitive and physically demanding theatre of the war. Robbins had joined the squadron as a green second lieutenant fresh out of training at Foster AAF, Texas; he had survived running-in on the Bell P-400 Aircobra and then with his unit had moved on to the vastly more capable Lockheed P-38. Twenty-four months later he was a major and deputy commander of the 8th Fighter Group and had collected twenty-two victories in air combat, along with several high decorations for valor and airmanship.

With *High Noon Over Alicante*, Roy Grinnell has chosen to depict Jay "Cock" Robbins' twenty-second and last aerial victory, the destruction of a Japanese Army Ki 43 Oscar over Alicante Airfield on Negros Island in the Philippines. This came at 1215 on 14 November while Robbins was leading eleven P-38s of the 36th Fighter Squadron as cover for a B-24 strike against Alicante. Flying top cover about sixteen thousand feet (4,800m), Robbins' *Blue Flight* sighted a Zero and three Oscars at about eight thousand feet (2,400m), apparently descending for a landing. The four P-38s released their drop tanks and dove on the Japanese; Robbins selected the leading Oscar as his target and hammered it with his 20mm cannon and four .50 cal. guns. Pieces flew off the lightly built Oscar, then a second burst shot off the canopy and set the plane afire before it smashed into the ground.

Scramble for the Marianas

Alexander "Alex" Vraciu, USN

Nicolas Trudgian

AT THE BEGINNING OF WORLD WAR II, THE BATTLESHIP WAS just what it had always been: the capital ship par excellence in all the world's navies. World War II, however, showed that the aircraft carrier, not the battleship, was the queen of naval battles; even the largest and most powerful battleships could fall victim to carrier-based air power. After 1945, battleships were relegated to coastal bombardment, while aircraft carriers continued to show ever-greater size, striking power, and operational efficiency.

Nicolas Trudgian's dramatic *Scramble for the Marianas* depicts a scene typical of U.S. Navy carrier operations during the high point of World War II in the Pacific. Steaming head-on into the wind, the USS *Lexington* launches a Grumman F6F-3 Hellcat from VF-16 "Fighting Airedales" off on a combat flight during the Battle of the Philippine Sea, 19–20 June, 1944. With flaps lowered and engine howling against a full load of fuel and ammunition, the Hellcat has accelerated from 0 to about 160 mph (256kph) in about half a deck length, or about four hundred feet (120m).

The aircraft portrayed in Trudgian's painting is that of Lt.(j.g.) Alex Vraciu, leading ace of the *Lexington*'s VF-16 "Fighting Airedales" in mid-1944. Born on 2 November, 1918, Vraciu had graduated from DePaul University with a B.A. in 1941. He was commissioned as an ensign following completion of flight training with the U.S. Navy in August 1942. During 1943 and early 1944 he was assigned to VF-6 "Shooting Stars" on the USS *Intrepid*, where he flew as wingman to squadron commander "Butch" O'Hare. Vraciu was assigned to VF-16 on the *Lexington* in February 1944; by mid-June he had accumulated twelve air victories. The Battle of the Philippine Sea would bring him seven more victories and a recommendation for the Medal of Honor, eventually reduced to an award of the Navy Cross.

Alex Vraciu shot down six enemy planes in one day during the legendary Marianas "Turkey Shoot" on 19 June, 1944. He claimed another the following day, and finished the war with a formidable nineteen victories.

The Marianas Turkey Shoot

Alexander "Alex" Vraciu, USN

Roy Grinnell

THE MARIANAS "TURKEY SHOOT" OF 19 JUNE, 1944, HAS A UNIQUE AND unchallenged place in the history of air warfare—it was the single greatest air battle of all time in terms of the number of planes lost. The stage for "the Shoot" was set after 15 June, 1944, when American troops landed on Saipan in the Marianas archipelago. The Imperial Japanese Navy reacted by sending its powerful First Mobile Fleet under Vice-Admiral Jisaburo Ozawa northeast out of the Philippine Sea on a do-or-die operation to save Saipan. Its target was Admiral Raymond Spruance's Task Force 58, operating west of Saipan with fifteen fleet and light carriers grouped into four task groups.

During the afternoon of 18 June, Japanese scout planes sighted TF 58 about two hundred miles (320km) west of Saipan, and early the next morning Admiral Ozawa's nine carriers put more than three hundred planes into the air to destroy it. Ozawa's massive attack, however, was doomed virtually from the outset: his 430 aircraft were outnumbered more than two-to-one, his air crew were less experienced than the Americans, and many of his aircraft were inferior to the U.S. Navy's F6F Hellcats, TBF Avengers, and Curtiss Helldivers.

What unfolded during the forenoon and afternoon of 19 June, 1944, was an unprecedented massacre of Japanese naval aviation that forever ended it as a effective fighting force. By the end of the day, 243 Japanese planes had hit the water at a cost of thirty-one American aircraft, a kill ratio of almost eight to one. Most Japanese aircraft types suffered badly, but the Yokosuka D4Y Judy single-engine bomber seemed to offer the turkey's choicest slices—Ozawa's carriers had embarked 174 Judys, of which fifty-seven, or nearly one in three, were shot down. In one wild spree before noon, Lt.(j.g.) Alex Vraciu from the USS *Lexington*'s VF-16 claimed six D4Y Judy bombers in quick succession, an action that would help bring him an award of the Navy Cross. Roy Grinnell's *The Marianas Turkey Shoot* depicts Vraciu's destruction of two of these Judys, while a third seems unable to take any evasive action and will doubtless soon become another victim in the Marianas shooting gallery.

On board the USS Lexington, pilots of the VF-16 "Fighting Airedales" grin across the wing of an F6F Hellcat after shooting down a total of twenty Japanese planes during one attack on Saipan in the Marianas. By the end of the famed "Turkey Shoot," more than two hundred Japanese planes had been destoyed.

One for the Big Friends
Francis S. "Gabby" Gabreski, USAAF

Roy Grinnell

DOZENS OF FIGHTER GROUPS IN THE EUROPEAN THEATRE OF OPERATIONS flew the P-47, but none was more closely identified with Republic's monster than the immortal 56th FG, the only Eighth AF group to keep Thunderbolts till war's end. And among the many outstanding 56th FG personalities, none outshines Francis S. "Gabby" Gabreski, third-ranking American ace of all time, top U.S. ace in the ETO, and all-time highest scorer in P-47s. Gabreski commanded the 56th's 61st FS between June 1943 and January 1944 and again between 13 April and 20 July, 1944. On 20 July, 1944 he decided to fly a last mission—his 166th—before going Stateside to be married. On return, however, he dropped to the deck to make a strafing run on a German airfield. Lining up on an He 111, he got too low, grazed a rise in the ground, bent the propeller, and crash-landed, becoming a POW after five days of evading capture.

Roy Grinnell's *One for the Big Friends* captures Gabreski's destruction of a Me 210 on 30 January, 1944, while the 56th FG was escorting Eighth AF bombers—"big friends" to the fighters—against Braunschweig. It was his tenth air victory. The Thunderbolt in the painting is s/n 42-75510, a Farmingdale-built P-47D-RE-11, which Gabreski flew between December 1943 and May 1944 and was presumably flying on 30 January, 1944. A photograph in Gabreski's 1991 autobiography, *Gabby: A Fighter Pilot's Story*, indicates that this airplane later (March 1944 onwards) sported the 56th FG's bright red cowling and also had a red rudder, the identifying color for the 61st FS. Following common Eighth AF practice for a fighter squadron commander, it carried the individual aircraft letter "A" with the 61st FS's HV- code, and several miniature German crosses were displayed under the cockpit on the port side.

First Strike on Berlin

B-17s - 100th Bomb Group vs. II./JG I, GAF

Nicolas Trudgian

ON 5 MARCH 1944, THE EIGHTH AIR FORCE REACHED A WATERSHED IN its strategic air offensive by launching its first operation against the capital of the Reich. But on the weather was uncooperative, and the Eighth had to try again the next day. On 6 March, one of the most historic days in the annals of air warfare, the Eighth dispatched some 730 heavy bombers against Berlin, escorted by 796 fighters from the Eighth and Ninth AF and the RAF—a column stretching for sixty miles (97km) across German skies. This force reached its objective and rained 1,648 tons (1,494t) of bombs on industrial targets in and around the city.

The air battle that unfolded during the first Berlin mission was ferocious. Of the 702 B-17s and B-24s that reached the Reich, sixty-nine—nearly one bomber in ten—did not return, and another four were fit only for scrap. The Luftwaffe, too, suffered badly, with some sixty-six fighters destroyed and twenty-four damaged. By day's end the bombers' track across northwestern Europe was littered with aircraft debris, collapsed parachutes, smoking holes, and airmen contemplating their futures as prisoners of war.

Of all Eighth AF bomber groups, none suffered more than the 100th BG, appropriately dubbed "the Bloody Hundredth." The 100th had launched thirty-six B-17s from Thorpe Abbotts, but six had aborted, leaving thirty to carry on. At 1155—about an hour short of Berlin—its B-17s were savagely set upon by JG 1 and other fighter units over Haselünne, Germany. Within one minute, all six bombers from the 100th's high squadron had been shot down. Others followed in the ensuing moments. The group's agony did not end completely until about 1600, when the pitiful remains of what once had been a proud formation straggled back to Thorpe Abbotts. Fifteen B-17s finally landed, every other one firing red flares for wounded aboard. This blow had cost JG 1, the main assailants over Haselünne, seven Fw 190s destroyed and five damaged out of fifty-four aircraft on strength.

The next day the Eighth did not fly because of weather, but on the 8th the 100th BG was again ordered to Berlin. It could put up only fifteen airplanes, of which one did not return.

COLONEL KENNETH R. MARTIN

Colonel Kenneth R. Martin, an ace with five victories, commanded a P-51 group in the Ninth Air Force. He scored his fifth victory during his final mission of the war, shooting down a Messerschmitt Me 410 on 11 February, 1944, before colliding with another German fighter. He parachuted safely but was taken prisoner. When Martin failed to return, he was replaced as group commander by Lieutenant Colonel James Howard, a former Flying Tiger, who on 11 January, 1944 had earned the Medal of Honor for breaking up an attack by German fighters on an Eighth Air Force bomber formation.

Clash of Eagles

Capt. Joe Bennett, USAAF

Roy Grinnell

ROY GRINNELL'S CLASH OF EAGLES IS A SPECTACULAR STOP-FRAME FROM the howling, no-quarter maelstrom that is the dogfight. In this case, it is a violent intersection in the careers of Capt. Joseph H. Bennett of the USAAF's 4th FG, 336th FS, and of Obfhr. Hubert Heckmann of the Luftwaffe's 9./JG 1. At the time of their clash, Bennett was a seasoned pilot with 6.5 victories who had already served seven months with the 56th FG before joining the 4th FG on 4 April 1944. Eleven days later, he had been forced to bail out into the North Sea after a mid-air collision but was fished out of the freezing water by a RAF Walrus. Injured, Bennett did not return to ops until several days later, only to shortly undergo another hair-raising experience.

On 25 May 1944 Bennett's three-man flight of P-51s ran into a formation of Bf 109Gs from III./JG 1 over Sarreguemines near the Franco-German frontier, and the American found himself locked in mortal combat with Obfhr. Heckmann, a grimly tenacious—some might say foolhardy—foe. When the guns of Heckmann's Bf 109G-6/AS yellow 15-I jammed, the German refused to let his quarry escape. Pulling up his Messerschmitt's nose, he caught Bennett's P-51B-7-NA s/n 43-6572 coded VF-N in a mighty Daimler-Benz buzzsaw that sliced off the Mustang's entire tail section. The American's aircraft madly whirled out of control, but the pilot baled out unhurt to become a prisoner of war. Released at war's end, Bennett was eventually credited with 8.5 victories and was awarded three Distinguished Flying Crosses.

Following his collision with the American, Heckmann successfully belly-landed his Bf 109G-6/AS (WNr. 163 796) near Botenheim. Returning to duty with his unit, he was injured in air combat with a P-38 followed by a crash landing near Compiègne, France, on 5 August 1944. He returned to duty, later flew Me 262s with JG 7, and survived the war with five victories.

Big Beautiful Doll
Col. J. D. Landers, USAF

Stan Stokes

MANY STUDENTS OF WORLD WAR II CLAIM THAT THE P-51 MUSTANG WAS the finest all-around propeller-driven fighter of the conflict, though this opinion is not shared by all. Fast, pilot-friendly, long-ranging, and reliable, the P-51 also had sufficient maneuverability and firepower to make it the fighter most feared by the Luftwaffe. These qualities were well appreciated in the Pentagon and by field commanders; by the end of the war, Mustangs had replaced every P-38 Lightning group and all but one P-47 Thunderbolt group in the Eighth AF. Others might venture that whatever looks good will probably fly well, and certainly the P-51's handsome lines fulfilled this expectation, too.

The Mustang that Stan Stokes has portrayed flying over a European village is P-51D-20-NA s/n 44-72218, built at North Amercan's Inglewood, California, plant in January 1945 and delivered to the Eighth Air Force in early February. Following its arrival in England, the airplane was assigned to the 78th FG at AAF Station Duxford, where service personnel turned her into a colorfully painted lady. They applied the 78th FG's unmistakable black-and-white checkerboard with red trim, then painted the rudder black and added the code letters WZ-I for the 84th FS. As such, s/n 44-72218 became the personal mount of Lt. Col. John D. Landers, 78th FG commander. Col. Landers kept up a personal custom by naming his ship *Big Beautiful Doll*, and maintenance personnel added Landers' name on the cockpit frame, along with six miniature Japanese and several Nazi flags tallying the pilot's aerial victories. While flying as 78th FG commander between 22 February and 28 June, 1945, Landers shot down at least two Bf 109s and shared in the destruction of a Me 262 with *Big Beautiful Doll*.

Like most American airplanes overseas at war's end, *Big Beautiful Doll* was thought too expensive to bring home. She was condemned to salvage and sold for scrap during the summer of 1945, having done short but faithful service to her pilot and her country.

Bridge Busting Jugs
56th Fighter Group and the P-47

Stan Stokes

STAN STOKES' *BRIDGE BUSTING JUGS* REPRESENTS TWO REPUBLIC P-47 Thunderbolts from the 56th FG attacking a railroad bridge in mountainous country in France some time after D-Day. This sort of mission was typical for thousands of Eighth and Ninth AF P-47s from the spring of 1944 until war's end—the USAAF had no aircraft more suitable for precise dive bombing and ground support than the robust, hard-hitting "Jug."

The 56th FG was unquestionably the most famous Thunderbolt unit in the Eighth AF. Throughout the war it flew escort missions for Eighth AF heavy bomber raids, but for a time after D-Day it carried out bridge-busting and other tactical missions in support of the Allied beachhead in Normandy. Most such attacks, however, were conducted in the flat or rolling country of northern and central France; P-47 units in Italy commonly operated in mountainous terrain such as that shown in the painting, but the 56th FG seldom did.

The 56th FG was comprised the 61st, 62nd, and 63rd Fighter Squadrons, each of which had its own distinctive code letters and rudder colors. The Thunderbolts shown in Stokes' painting belong to the 61st FS, whose squadron code was "H V" followed by an individual aircraft letter. Each airplane also carries the brilliant red cowling adopted by the 56th after March 1944. The painting depicts the planes operating in the weeks immediately following D-Day, for they still display the unmistakable white-and-black identification stripes that were applied to all Allied tactical aircraft on 5 June. These stripes would gradually be removed during the late summer and fall of 1944.

FRANCIS GABRESKI

Francis Gabreski was the top American ace in air-to-air victories over Europe during World War II; he was officially credited with twenty-eight. While he was strafing a German airfield on 20 July, 1944, the propeller on his P-47 struck the ground and Gabreski had to crash-land. He was captured and sent to *Stalag Luft 1* near Barth, Germany, where he spent the remainder of the war. He returned to combat during the Korean Conflict where he scored an additional 6.5 victories. Gabreski retired from the USAAF as a Colonel in October 1967, America's top living ace.

A Pair of Aces

Richard I. Bong and Thomas B. McGuire, USAAF

Stan Stokes

BY HAPPENSTANCE, THE TWO HIGHEST RANKING ACES OF THE USAAF DURING World War II both came from the Pacific Theatre and both flew P-38 Lightnings; on occasion, they even served in the same unit.

Richard I. "Dick" Bong joined the 49th FG, 9th FS, in the southwest Pacific late in 1942 and a year later had run up twenty-one victories and several probables. After forty days' leave beginning in November 1943, he returned to the Southwest Pacific on a roving assignment with the V Fighter Command, where he ran his score up to forty with several probables before war's end. On 8 December, 1944, Bong received the Medal of Honor from Gen. Douglas MacArthur. When the Pacific War ended in August 1945, Bong became the highest ranking American fighter ace of all time, but he had little time to enjoy this prestige before he died testing a Lockheed P-80A on 6 August, 1945.

Thomas B. "Tommy" McGuire was assigned to the 475th FG, 431st FS, in mid-July 1943, having previously served in the Aleutians and with the 49th FG, 9th FS. He remained with the 431st FS in the southwest Pacific until 7 January, 1945, when he was killed in combat while attempting to snap roll onto the tail of a Japanese Zero without dropping his external fuel tank. The mistake sent McGuire into a flat spin from which he was unable to recover, or even bail out. Prior to his death, McGuire ran up thirty-eight aerial victories and several probables, a tally that permanently established him as the second-highest ranked American fighter ace of all time (after Bong). McGuire was posthumously awarded the Medal of Honor in 1946.

Bong's roving assignment with V FC during 1944 allowed him to choose the units he wanted to fly with, and on 7 December, 1944, he flew a mission with McGuire and two other members of the 431st FS. Although Bong and McGuire were intense rivals and did not fly as wingmen on 7 December, Stan Stokes has captured a moment when the aircraft of America's two highest aces were wing-to-wing. The Lightning in the foreground without unit markings is Dick Bong's P-38J-15-LO s/n 42-104380 (*Marge*); the aircraft to Bong's starboard is Tommy McGuire's P-38L-1-LO s/n 44-24155 (*Pudgy*, fifth of this name) with individual aircraft no. 131 and squadron commander's stripes.

Showdown Over Berrière

Kenneth H. Dahlberg, USAAF

Roy Grinnell

On 2 June, 1944, first Lt. Kenneth H. Dahlberg joined the 353rd FS of the 354th FG in England as a replacement pilot, one of hundreds of new air crew flowing into American units weekly. At this stage of the war all of these newcomers were well trained, but Dahlberg was exceptionally so: his logbook showed 1,015 and one-half hours flying time as contrasted with the 200 to 300 hours typical of the newly minted American pilot and the sixty to eighty characteristic of his German opposite. This seasoning would soon serve the newly arrived lieutenant well.

For the first two weeks or so of his tour, Dahlberg had relatively few chances to engage the enemy, but they increased notably after mid-June, when the 354th FG moved across the Channel and established itself on a temporary airfield near Criqueville. The forward deployment put the 354th's squadrons close to the front lines, multiplying the daily missions flown and thus the chance to tangle with the Luftwaffe.

On 22 June, Dahlberg claimed his first aerial victory, a Bf 109 near Rambouillet. Exactly a week later, he was able to claim his second German, a Fw 190, during an early afternoon fighter sweep behind German lines. Shortly past 1400 on 29 June, Dahlberg's flight encountered a large number of Fw 190s over Berrière, and a swirling dogfight ensued. One of the Focke Wulfs turned in behind his flight leader's tail; Dahlberg caught the German in his gunsight and fired a burst that caused the enemy to break off. A writhing, twisting, turning fight for life followed as both fighters tried to maneuver for position. With the combat nearly down to tree-top level, Dahlberg finally fired a fatal burst and the German dove into the ground. Dahlberg later described this German pilot as his most formidable air opponent—perhaps because he may have come from JG 26, one of the Luftwaffe's best fighter units in the West.

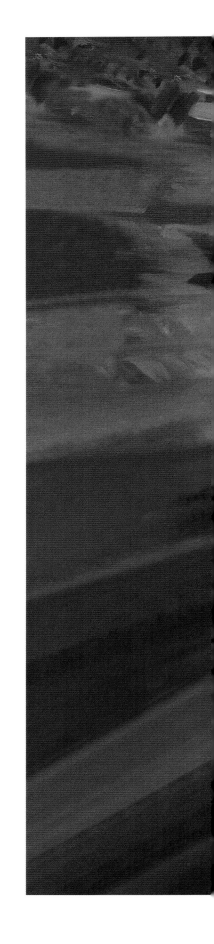

Lightning Over Leyte
Charles H. MacDonald, USAAF

Mike Machat

Of the top three USAAF fighters of World War II—the P-38 Lightning, the P-47 Thunderbolt, and the P-51 Mustang—the Lockheed P-38 certainly had the most distinctive personality. Its twin boom-central cockpit configuration made it instantly recognizable any time, any place—there was no confusing this airplane with a Spitfire or a Fw 190. The Lightning also had its own well-defined characteristics: very fast up to 18,000 feet (5,000m) or so, it possessed a powerful, centrally grouped gun package; long range; tricycle landing gear; and the security that two engines provided. Unfortunately, Lockheed's engineers could not repeal the laws of physics, and while quite maneuverable, the heavy twin-engined P-38 could never turn and roll like a single-engined fighter, especially at higher altitudes where its Allison engines lost out to the competition.

In the end, all of the P-38's virtues could not redeem it in Europe, but the Pacific was a different matter. There, with some allowance for tactics, the P-38 proved itself to be very nearly the ideal fighter. It alone, for example, could have carried out the interception of Admiral Yamamoto on 18 April, 1943. No P-38 fighter group made better use of the Lightning's traits than the 475th FG, which during 1944 operated from Hollandia and Biak, then from October 1944 out of various bases in the Philippines. The 475th's achievements were outstanding; the unit's rosters included both Dick Bong and Tommy McGuire, the two highest ranked USAAF aces of the war. The group was also host to Charles Lindbergh during his southwest Pacific "tour of duty" in the summer of 1944.

Much of the 475th's success can be credited to Charles H. MacDonald, who twice commanded the group and impressed his own high standards on it. Flying a series of P-38s named *Putt Putt Maru*, MacDonald routinely led demanding long-range over-water missions and ran up a personal score of twenty-seven victories by war's end. Mike Machat's *Lightning Over Leyte* portrays MacDonald's destruction of a Mitsubishi J2M6 Raiden over Luzon on 25 December, 1944, one of three certain and one probable victories by him on that mission.

Return to Halesworth

Walker M. "Bud" Mahurin, USAAF

Gil Cohen

GIL COHEN'S ART IS DISTINGUISHED BY ITS FOCUS ON PEOPLE; *Return to Haleworth* is true to form. The picture catches 56th FG ace Walker "Bud" Mahurin being congratulated by ground personnel on the hardstand at AAF Station Halesworth after a mission, probably during late 1943.

Bud Mahurin was one of a storied group of aces within the Eighth AF's 56th FG, including Gabreski, Zemke, Schilling, Robert S. Johnson, and Gerald Johnson. He joined the group's 63rd FS in England in January 1943 and scored steadily from that time until 27 March, 1944, when he was shot down by the rear gunner of a Dornier Do 217 about fifteen miles (24km) south of Chartres, France. The Dornier subsequently became his twentieth and final victory with the 56th. Mahurin evaded capture with the help of French partisans and finally

returned to the United Kingdom on 7 May, 1944. Denied permission to fly in Europe again because of security considerations, he was transferred to the 3rd Air Commando Group in the southwest Pacific, where he gained one additional air victory before the war ended. He remained in the USAAF postwar, and flew in Korea, where he achieved several victories until he was shot down, and this time taken prisoner. He did not return to the United States until September 1953.

The aircraft shown in *Return to Halesworth* is P-47D-5-RE s/n 42-8487, which Mahurin used regularly between September 1943 and March 1944. This Thunderbolt carried the name *Spirit of Atlantic City* on the fuselage sides; the name was not a personal marking but indicated that the machine had been presented by the people of Atlantic City, New Jersey.

Lindbergh's Secret

Charles A. Lindbergh, USAAF

Domenic DeNardo

TRIVIA LOVERS, HERE'S A WORLD WAR II STUMPER: WHICH AMERICAN FLEW combat missions as a civilian and actually shot down an enemy plane while doing so? Answer: Charles A. Lindbergh! And yes, that's the same Charles Lindbergh of 1927 Atlantic solo crossing–fame and the same Lindbergh who married writer and poet Anne Morrow.

In reality, Lindbergh's combat experience was scarcely trivial. Although he possessed enormous aviation expertise and had been a colonel in the U.S. Army Air Corps Reserve, Lindbergh was never called to active duty during World War II. This may have been because of his public and powerfully articulated opposition to America's entry into the war. Both the Ford Motor Company and United Aircraft Corporation, however, engaged Lindbergh as a technical consultant, and in 1944 the U.S. Navy granted him permission to investigate problems with the F4U/FG Corsair. In mid-June 1944 he proceeded to the Army Air Forces' 5th Fighter Command headquarters at Nadzab, New Guinea. Here, Lindbergh wrangled permission to visit a frontline P-38 outfit in order to observe the Lightning's performance under combat conditions. Although he had never flown a P-38 before, he was quickly checked out in the fighter, and a few days later flew a short combat mission with the 8th FG, 35th FS.

Although Charles Lindbergh resigned his colonel's commission with the Army Air Corps Reserve in 1941 amid controversy over his opposition to the war, he did fly a number of missions as a civilian with the 457th fighter group.

Leaving Nadzab in a P-38 on 26 June, Lindbergh flew to Hollandia, New Guinea, where he made an extended visit with the 475th FG, also equipped with P-38s. Between 26 June and 16 August, "Lucky Lindy" went on an undisclosed but significant number of combat missions with the 475th FG; during one such sortie with group commander Col. Charles MacDonald's *Blue Flight* on 28 July, Lindbergh shot down a Ki 51 Sonia reconnaissance plane over the southern coast of Ceram. The USAAF never gave Lindbergh official credit for the Sonia, but his "combat tour" did produce important lessons about how the average pilot should manage fuel in the big fighter, resulting in an extension of its range by up to 30 percent.

Guardian Angels

78th Fighter Group, USAAF

Jim Laurier

TO THE FORTRESS AND LIBERATOR CREWS OF THE EIGHTH AF, THE Lightnings, Thunderbolts, and Mustangs weaving overhead and to either side were their "little friends," the fighter escorts that alone could keep the Luftwaffe at arm's length. Until January 1943, the "little friends" had had short legs and could only play guardian angel for a few hundred miles from England before turning back. The Eighth's heavy bomber losses during 1943 reflected this situation—the horrific first and second Schweinfurt missions, the Bremen raid of 8 October, the Münster operation on 10 October, and other costly operations at the close of that year were directly attributable to a lack of long-range fighter escorts.

In January 1944, however, the air war took a radical turn when Eighth AF P-51 Mustangs began using drop tanks so they could accompany their "big friends" all the way to the target area. From this point on the Luftwaffe was doomed. The advent of escort fighters with drop tanks was the single most important factor in destroying the German Air Force during the spring of 1944. During 1944 the P-51 Mustang with drop tanks became the Eighth AF's escort fighter par excellence, and by the summer of 1944 the Eighth had ten Mustang groups that could send five hundred fighters anywhere the bombers could fly.

The 78th FG featured in Jim Laurier's *Guardian Angels* had begun operations with P-38s from AAF Station Goxhill early in 1943, but in April it moved to Duxford, its home for the rest of the war. The group received P-47 Thunderbolts in June 1943, then converted to P-51s at the end of December 1944. By war's end the group had been awarded two Distinguished Unit Citations for operations over Holland in 1944 and over Czechoslovakia in 1945.

In *Guardian Angels* a flight of P-51s from the 78th FG patrols high above B-17 "big friends" from the 1st Air Division sometime after February 1945. The flight leader—the second P-51 from the left—is WZ -I *Big Beautiful Doll*, the aircraft of 78th FG commander Col. John D. Landers.

Hostile Sky

USAAF versus the Luftwaffe, 1944

Robert Taylor

ROBERT TAYLOR'S HOSTILE SKY DEPICTS A GENERIC SCENE REPEATED MANY times in west European skies during 1944 and 1945. A crippled B-24 Liberator from the 392nd BG has been forced to leave the protective fold of its formation; engine smoking, it has turned for home by itself. Two P-38 Lightnings have been detailed to see the damaged bomber home, if they can. It is a tough assignment, because Luftwaffe fighters like nothing more than to find and finish off such an isolated cripple, and two "little friends" could scarcely hold off a swarm of determined attackers.

As is usual with Taylor paintings, the composition of *Hostile Sky* is supremely fitting and transcends the obvious. The first and overwhelming impression that one gets is one of fear and utter chaos; the wounded "big friend" banks away just as two Fw 190As bore in for the kill. Simultaneously, two P-38 "little friends" make a head-on pass to try to thwart the German attack.

The distribution of shapes and angles is tense and beautifully captures the wild and often uncoordinated ballet of air combat.

Twilight Conquest

Orvis B. Johnson, USAAF

Nicolas Trudgian

THE USAAF NEVER RAISED A LARGE NIGHT FIGHTING PRESENCE IN EUROPE during World War II; in fact, only two American night fighter squadrons, the 422nd and 425th, operated in the European Theatre. In large measure, this was because the RAF had long and deep experience in all kinds of night operations, but it was also because American preparation for night air war came late and was handicapped by inferior aircraft. From 1941 to 1943, the United States had thought little about air fighting in darkness, and it had no night fighters like the Bristol Beaufighter or the superb De Havilland DH 98 Mosquito. The Northrop P-61 Black Widow, a night fighter designed from scratch, did not become operational in England until June 1944, and even then it demonstrated a marked inferiority to the British Mosquito. For these reasons, there were only three American night fighter aces in the ETO, all from the 422nd NFS.

One of the relatively few American air victories at night came on 24 October, 1944, when Lt. Col. Orvis B. Johnson, commander of the 422nd NFS, claimed a Fw 190A near Aachen, Germany, flying P-61A s/n 42-5558. Johnson's claim came after the 9th Tactical Air Command observed a pattern in which Luftwaffe fighters would come up at dusk, cross the Rhine, and make a fast hit-and-run against American forces. It was decided to put up two-aircraft patrols over the Köln-Ostheim-Wahn-Bonn sector beginning about a half hour before darkness with the hope of foiling these raiders. On 24 October, these tactics succeeded as Lt. Col. Johnson's radar operator found a formation of three Fw 190s. Johnson stalked them and at 1818 blasted one of the trio. It was the 422nd's second aerial victory.

Yeager's First Jet

Charles E. "Chuck" Yeager, USAAF

Roy Grinnell

Chuck Yeager finished out World War II with no fewer than eleven aerial victories, all of them aboard P-51 Mustangs dubbed *Glamorous Glenn* after his wife, Glennis.

THE MESSERSCHMITT ME 262 WAS THE MOST TECHNOLOGICALLY ADVANCED fighter to see combat during World War II. With a top speed well above 500 miles per hour (800kph), no Allied fighter could catch it, so the German jet could usually dictate the terms of combat, or even whether there would be a fight at all. There was, however, one window of vulnerability with the Me 262: during take-off and landing the jet's primitive turbines had to be throttled very carefully, making sudden acceleration and evasive action virtually impossible. Caught in the landing or take-off regime, the jet became easy prey for roving USAAF and RAF foes.

The USAAF discovered the Me 262's Achilles' heel almost as soon as the jet went into operations with *Kommando Nowotny* at the beginning of November 1944. On the 6th of November, Capt. Charles E. "Chuck" Yeager's Cement White flight of the 357th FG encountered several of the Me 262s previously rumored to be active in the Osnabrück area, but owing to their speed and to hazy conditions, the jets escaped when first attacked. A few minutes later, however, Yeager sighted one of the Germans approaching his home field at about 200 miles per hour (320kph), closed to within four hundred yards (360m), and fired a short burst. Intense airfield flak then drove the American off, but Yeager was able to see the German jet crash-land and its right wing come off. This Me 262 became Yeager's first and only confirmed jet victory, but he was able to claim two others as damaged during the same mission.

Steinhoff Tribute

Johannes "Macky" Steinhoff, Luftwaffe

Robert Taylor

IN COMPANY WITH A SMALL NUMBER OF HIS PEERS DURING WORLD WAR II, Johannes "Macky" Steinhoff was first and last a professional soldier, an officer, and a leader of men, though with 176 air victories he also ranked twenty-second among the greatest aces of all time. He initially enlisted in the *Kriegsmarine* for officer's training in 1934 but quickly transferred to the Luftwaffe and spent the remainder of his career in the air arm. Between 1939 and 1945 he flew with a number of fighter units, including JG 26, JG 52, JG 77, NJG 1, and the elite jet unit JV 44. By war's end, Steinhoff had risen to *Oberstleutnant* and wore the Knight's Cross with Oak Leaves and Swords; his leadership abilities might well have made him a general had he not fallen out with Hermann Goering and participated in a protest critical of the *Reichsmarschall* in early 1945, which foreclosed any chance of further advancement. Steinhoff was apparently a man of enormous spirit, fortitude, and self-will: terribly burned and disfigured in a Me 262 accident in April 1945, he spent months in the hospital, recovered something of a normal existence and appearance, was accepted into the Bundes Luftwaffe in the mid-50s, and rose to the rank of general before his retirement in 1972.

Robert Taylor's *Steinhoff Tribute* depicts a Bf 109E as flown by Steinhoff of 4./JG 52 during the Battle of Britain. The white cliffs of Dover need no comment, while the Hurricanes banking below Steinhoff belong to no. 32 Squadron.

Johannes Steinhoff transferred to the *Luftwaffe* from the navy in 1934. He started the war flying the Me 109 and gained the last of his victories in the Me 262 jet. He fought on almost every front, scoring 149 kills against Soviet airmen and twenty-seven against the French and British.

Thunderbolt Strike

P-47 Thunderbolt and the 404th FG

Robert Taylor

REPUBLIC'S P-47 THUNDERBOLT WAS ARGUABLY ONE OF THE TOP THREE USAAF fighters of World War II. It found employment in every theatre of war, but the greatest number of Thunderbolts made their way to the European Theatre of Operations, where thousands served as escort fighters for the Eighth AF and as fighter-bombers for the Ninth AF. In any role, the Thunderbolt had a character all its own, that of an awesome juggernaut (hence the moniker "Jug") with wings. At more than six tons (5.4t) loaded, a Thunderbolt could dive like nothing else; with a burly 2000 hp. Pratt & Whitney R-2800 radial engine swinging a four-bladed 13-foot (3.9m) propeller, it could hold its own in climb; under water injection boost, it could catch or outrace almost all Luftwaffe fighters; and with eight 0.50 cal. guns, it could instantly shred any aerial or ground target. If the P-47 had any shortcoming, it was its thirst, which limited its range, even with drop tanks.

During 1943 and early 1944, the P-47 served as the mainstay escort for Eighth AF's B-17s and B-24s, whose crews called them the heavy bomber's "little friends." As large numbers of P-51 Mustangs came on line during 1944, however, an increasing proportion of P-47s were assigned to the Ninth AF as fighter-bombers, a less glamorous but vital role they played without peer till war's end. With its immense power, the P-47 could lift two 500- or even 1000-lb. (225 or 450kg) bombs and deliver them precisely, while its eight 0.50 cal. machine guns made it a fearsome strafing machine. Its solidity gave its pilots supreme confidence, even in the dangerous light flak environment fifty to one hundred feet (15 to 30m) above the ground.

Robert Taylor's *Thunderbolt Strike* depicts a formation of P-47D fighter-bombers of the 404th Fighter Group outbound from a post–D-Day strike in northern France. The nearest "Jug" has been holed by small-arms fire but flies on, while seagulls flee in terror from the pounding engines invading their territory.

Photo Finish

F-6 and Photo Reconnaissance, USAAF

Mike Machat

IT LOOKS LIKE AN ORDINARY NORTH AMERICAN P-51 MUSTANG, BUT IT ISN'T: Mike Machat's *Photo Finish* represents a special type of P-51, the F-6 photo reconnaissance version. Converted from a standard P-51 and virtually identical to it, the F-6 offered a superb long-distance photo-reconnaissance capability while maintaining all the lethal qualities of the fighter version.

Although able to a degree to defend themselves, F-6 pilots normally sought to avoid encounters with enemy aircraft. Their job was to get in, get pictures, and get away with the precious film, a responsibility the good photo-rec pilot always kept foremost in his mind. Sometimes, however, photo-rec pilots stretched the rules, and occasionally, there was no choice but to shoot one's way out. One way or another Clyde B. East of the 10th Photo Reconnaissance Group, 15th Tactical Reconnaissance Squadron, Eighth AF, had his share of

scrapes; by war's end he was a photo-rec ace with no fewer than thirteen victories to his credit.

On 8 April, 1945, it was a matter of an alluring opportunity for East, who could not resist deviating from his mission when he sighted a lone Heinkel He 111H northeast of Dresden, Germany. Operating with air supremacy within weeks of war's end, East felt confident enough to jump the hapless Heinkel and shoot it down. Watching the bomber make a dead stick landing in a cabbage patch, East then flew a pass over the scene with the cameras running in *Lil' Margaret* (F-6 s/n 44-14306, 5M-K) to authenticate the victory, his twelfth.

As a footnote, the 10th PRG claimed a total of eighty-seven aerial victories and several probables in the European Theatre. The group's 15th TRS produced three aces: East, J. H. Hcefker (8.5 victories), and L. A. Larson (6).

Danger, Lightning Nearby

Charles H. MacDcnald, USAAF

Roy Grinnell

DURING WORLD WAR II, A FEW USAAF FIGHTER UNITS BECAME CLOSELY associated with their commanders, usually veteran officers with unusual leadership qualities. Often, these commanders were themselves high-ranking aces who set standards of combat effectiveness by their own examples. Charles H. MacDonald—inseparably identified with the 475th FG—was such an officer.

MacDonald entered the Air Reserves after graduating from college in 1938, then transferred to USAAC, which commissioned him as a first lieutenant on 9 September, 1940. He was serving with the 18th Pursuit Group at Wheeler Field, Hawaii, when the Japanese attacked on 7 December, 1941, but, like most other American pilots, he did not get airborne that day. From 1941 on, MacDonald was promoted rapidly and by November 1942 he was a major commanding the 348th FG. He transferred to the 475th FG at the beginning of

October 1943 and led the group for eight months. Toward the end of this period, his unit hosted Charles Lindbergh's unofficial "tour of duty" in the southwest Pacific, a curious episode that turned sour for MacDonald when he was recalled to the United States in August 1944 for having permitted his civilian guest to fly combat missions. This enforced leave lasted two months, and MacDonald was restored to command of the 475th in October 1944, a post he held almost to war's end. By the time of the Japanese surrender, he had run up twenty-seven aerial victories and wore two Distinguished Service Crosses, two Silver Stars, and six Distinguished Flying Crosses.

Following the cessation of hostilities, MacDonald remained in the Air Force until July 1961, when he retired as a colonel. Warbird enthusiasts associate him with a series of P-38s, all numbered "100" and all named *Putt Putt Maru*.

Calm Before the Storm
The Men Who Kept 'Em Flying, USAAF

Jim Laurier

IN THE REALM OF AVIATION ART, THE PREVALENT SCENES ARE THOSE showing the airplane soaring in flight or locked in mortal combat. The unspoken message is usually high flight, historic drama, or glorious valor. With *Calm Before the Storm*, Jim Laurier ventured to be different—this painting honors the faceless, nameless thousands of maintenance personnel who kept the fighting forces in the air. Working as long as necessary at thankless and often routine or repetitive tasks, outdoors in heat, cold, rain, or frost, the technical specialists performed miracles of diagnosis and repair. Day-in and day-out, they muscled bombs, hung drop tanks, changed tires, cleaned and bore-sighted weapons, packed parachutes, and tested radios. At all times they carried the heavy responsibility of zero-defect safety for their charges, and mission after mission they sat suffering silently through the long hours while their planes and their pilots flew into the hell of enemy air space—"sweating out the mission," it was called.

The setting for *Calm Before the Storm* is a hardstand at AAF Station Boxted, Essex, England, home to seventy-five-plus P-47 Thunderbolts of the Eighth AF's 56th FG. It is early morning—perhaps 0630—in mid-June 1944, and the shadows are still long as an armorer stacks boxes of 0.50 cal. ammunition in front of the 62nd FS's LM-A and another technician meticulously cleans its windscreen. Lying on the ground is a drop tank waiting to be hung on the belly rack. Soon the fuel bowser will trundle up, hundreds of gallons of high-octane gasoline will be pumped in, and LM-A will once again be ready to fly and to fight.

CAPTAIN WALTER KRUPINSKI

Walter Krupinski, for whom Erich Hartmann served briefly as wingman, was for a time Germany's leading ace. He was transferred from the Soviet Union, where kills were comparatively easy, to defend Germany against American bombers. Facing better trained opposition, he could not maintain his earlier pace, and ended the war with 197 victories.

Too Little, Too Late

Messerschmitt Me 262, Luftwaffe

Stan Stokes

THE MESSERSCHMITT ME 262 WAS ONE OF THE MANY REMARKABLE products of Germany's relentless quest for technological innovation during World War II. First flown in 1942, the Me 262 was powered by two Junkers Jumo 004 axial flow turbine engines that could push it along at more than 525 mph (840kph), 50 mph (80kph) faster than any propeller-driven Allied fighter. Its armament of four 30mm cannon represented fearsome destructive power, but it also featured a number of other modern features such as a bubble canopy, tricycle landing gear, and, on occasion, underwing air-to-air rocket armament. Altogether, on paper the Me 262 was far and away the most technologically advanced and formidable fighter of World War II to see action in any numbers.

The airplane was a great engineering achievement, and had a tremendous psychological impact on Allied air forces, but its scary potential never came close to fulfillment—and probably never could have, given wartime conditions. Delayed by high-level bumbling, developmental problems, conflicts in tactical employment, and, above all, plagued by shortages of strategic materials, the Me 262 was always "too little, too late" to make any noticeable difference in the air war. It is, nevertheless, an enduring monument to Teutonic engineering and is highly significant as the world's first jet aircraft to go into combat.

Stan Stokes' *Too Little, Too Late* depicts a Me 262 making a fast pass on a B-24 Liberator sometime in late 1944. The Me 262 shown is marked like a trial aircraft and probably never saw combat.

Wie ein Floh, aber Oh…

("*Like a Flea, but Oh . . .*")

Messerschmitt Me 163 Komet

Mike Machat

HIGH OVER BOHLEN, GERMANY, ON 16 AUGUST, 1944, B-17 CREWMEN in the Eighth AF's 1st Air Division were astonished to see four of what appeared to be small propellerless flying wings dive at unbelievable speed through their formation. The weird shapes then repeated their act, closing to within two hundred yards (180m) before breaking off and disappearing. The sightings confirmed what had long been feared: the Luftwaffe had brought the world's first rocket-powered interceptor to operational status. Whispered dread began to spread throughout the Eighth's bomber crews. It was clear that nothing could match the Me 163's blinding speed, and its small size made it a near-impossible target; should these fiendish contrivances show up in numbers, no one could predict what would become of the bomber offensive.

The Allies' fears proved groundless. Over the ensuing months, a few Me 163 Komets came up during attacks on oil refineries at Leuna and Merseburg, but only a handful of bombers ever fell to the Komets. Indeed, the Me 163 was more dangerous to its own pilots than to the USAAF. It had no landing gear but depended on a releasable dolly for take-off and a skid for landing. The Komet's propulsion was also a nightmare, for its little Walter rocket motor depended on the spontaneous combustion of 30 percent hydrazine hydrate solution in methyl alcohol and 48 percent concentrated hydrogen peroxide—a leak or just mishandling a few drops could, and did, produce instantaneous bomb-like blasts. These technical problems and a flight duration of only twelve minutes kept the Komet from amounting to anything other than an amazing aerial curiosity.

Major R. Bruce Porter—
Marine Night Fighter Ace

Battle of Okinawa, 1945

Jim Laurer

MAJ. BRUCE PORTER'S CAREER AS A MARINE CORPS FLYER REALLY BEGAN with his comission as a second lieutenant and reception of the naval aviator's gold wings on 1 August, 1942. During 1942–1943 he served with VMF-121 in the Pacific and by mid-summer 1943 he had accumulated three victories and at least two probables flying the F4U-1 Corsair in the Solomons. Returning to the States, he served as executive officer for a succession of Marine fighter squadrons during 1944. Between 7–9 May, 1945, he led a remarkable long-distance flight of VMF(N)-533 F6F Hellcat night fighters from Engebi in the Marshall Islands to Saipan, thence to Iwo Jima, and finally on to Okinawa,

a total of 16.6 flight hours over water. Two weeks after arriving on Okinawa, Porter assumed command of VMF(N)-542, a Marine night fighter unit flying ultra-modern radar-equipped F6F-5N Hellcats against noctural Japanese intruders. This duty was extraordinarily demanding, since the pilot had to fly his powerful single-engined fighter on instruments while operating the air interception radar and watching its cathode ray display screen. Porter proved himself a master at this juggling act in darkness: on 15 June, 1945, he shot down a G4M Betty and a Kawasaki Ki 45 Nick in one mission, thereby making himself an ace and earning the Distinguished Flying Cross.

Eagles Over the Rhine

353rd Fighter Group, USAAF

Robert Taylor

IT IS OVER. VICTORIOUS AFTER NEARLY THREE YEARS AND COUNTLESS bloody air battles in Europe, one group from the Eighth AF stages its own victory parade over the Rhine River. Robert Taylor's *Eagles Over the Rhine* captures a flight of four P-51Ds at low altitude over the Rhenish town of Kaub, Germany, soon after the end of hostilities. The leading Mustang is s/n 44-73060, the *Dove of Peace* (LM-X) assigned to Col. Glenn E. Duncan. Duncan was group commander of the 353rd Fighter Group between November 1943 and July 1944 and again between April and September 1945, and finished the war with 19.5 victories. This *Dove of Peace* was the eighth aircraft Duncan so named, and it carries the 353rd FG's livery of black and yellow checkered engine cowlings and yellow-black striped spinners.

About the Artists

C.S. Bailey

C.S. Bailey prefers to work in airbrush, a medium that allows his creativity to soar. "What better way to paint aircraft than with air?" Bailey asks. He graduated from the University of Utah with a BFA in Fine Arts and have been airbrushing modern aircraft, World War II planes, and naval ships for more than twenty years. His paintings have been featured in such publications as *Flight* and *Aviation History* magazines, and have been exhibited at the American Fighter Aces Museum in Texas. Bailey was the featured artist for the Salt Lake Aviation Aerospace Expo '94. His painting *Just-a-Snapping: A Flying Fortress* served as a backdrop for the reunion of the crew of the World War II aircraft that inspired it. C.S. Bailey is a member of the American Society of Aviation Artists and the Oklahoma Aviation Artist Association, and actively participates in the U.S. Air Force Art Program.

For information or to order prints, call or write:
C.S. Bailey Studios
2066 Greenbriar Circle
Salt Lake City, UT 84109
tel: (800) 494-6904

Gil Cohen

For more than forty years, Gil Cohen has worked as a freelance illustrator and painter of historical subjects. A graduate of the Philadelphia College of Art (now the University of the Arts), his clients include the U.S. Information Agency, the National Park Service, Paramount Pictures, the U.S. Coast Guard, and Boeing and Sikorsky Aircraft Companies. Artist Fellow Cohen is a three-time Best of Show winner at American Society of Aviation Artists (ASAA) juried exhibitions, and is the recipient of the British Guild of Aviation Artists' Best of Show by an American artist. His paintings have been exhibited at the New York Society of Illustrators, at the Kennedy Center in Washington, D.C, and at numerous Civil War battlefield national parks. His painting *Staying Power/Berlin 1948–49* was presented to the Berlin Airlift Museum. He is currently on the Board of Directors of the New York–based Society of Illustrators, where he chairs the Government Services Program. Gil Cohen's studio is located in the home that he shares with his wife, Alice, and their four cats in historic Doylestown, Pennsylvania.

For information or to order prints, call or write:
Gil Cohen
62 Creek Drive
Doylestown, PA 18901-4717
tel: (215) 348-0779
fax: (215) 348-2746

Domenic DeNardo

Domenic DeNardo has always been fascinated with aircraft. A graduate of the Rhode Island School of Design, DeNardo is the founder of the Art Center Studio in Providence, Rhode Island. His work is centered on technical illustrations for advertising agencies and manufacturers, and can be seen in such publications as *Aviation Week & Space Technology*, *Time*, and *The Wall Street Journal*. His paintings have received numerous awards including the Experimental Aircraft Association's Award of Excellence, the J. Bennigan Sullivan Prize from the Providence Art Club, and the Peoples' Choice Award from the Cranston Cultural Arts Show of Rhode Island. His painting *Victory Bound* won the Award of Distinction from the SimuFlite/ *Flying* Magazine Horizons of Flight Competition. His paintings have been exhibited throughout the country, and he is a member of several aircraft and artist associations. DeNardo, along with his wife and three children, has enjoyed many flying adventures throughout the continental United States as well as Alaska, Canada, Mexico, and the Bahamas.

For information or to order prints, call or write:
The Art Center Studio
23 Jones Street
Providence, RI 02903
tel: (401) 421-2651
fax: (401) 421-2691

James Dietz

For James Dietz, simply illustrating aviation hardware is not presenting the whole picture; he prefers to add a human element to truly capture the moment in his paintings. "The people, settings, and costumes are what make aviation history exciting and romantic to me," says the artist. A graduate of the Art Center College of Design, he worked as a commercial illustrator in Los Angeles before moving to Seattle to pursue a career in aviation art. His clients include Boeing, Bell Helicopter, Allison, and Flying Tigers. His work has been honored with several gold medals from the Los Angeles Society of Illustrators and was voted Best of Show in three successive years in the Experimental Aircraft Association Aviation Art Show. His work has been exhibited in museums throughout the country, including the Experimental Aircraft Association Museum, the San Diego Air Museum, and the Smithsonian Institution's National Air and Space Museum. Dietz lives in Seattle with his wife, Patti, and their son, Ian.

For information or to order prints, call or write:
Heritage Aviation Art/Mail Order Department
12819 SE 38th Street, #211
Bellevue, Washington 98006
tel: (800) 331-9044
fax: (206) 747-7429

Keith Ferris

The son of a career air force officer, Keith Ferris nurtured his love for aeronautics while growing up on military bases throughout the United States. As a freelance aviation artist and founding member of the American Society of Aviation Artists (ASAA), he has been serving the advertising, editorial, public relations, and historical documentation needs of the aviation community for more than fifty years. His clients include the Air Force Association, Aircraft Owners and Pilots Association, and *Aviation Week & Space Technology* magazine. A life member of the Air Force Association, he was a recipient of its Citation of Honor in 1978 for his art and its special award in 1985 for his lifetime of air force history documentation. His painting *Real Trouble* was judged Best of Show at the 1995 ASAA annual exhibition. Best known for his seventy-five-foot (22.8m) murals *Fortresses Under Fire* and *The Evolution of Jet Aviation*, his work has been exhibited at the Smithsonian Institution in Washington, D.C. and the United States Air Force Academy in Colorado Springs, Colorado. In 1992, he was inducted into the Aviation Hall of Fame of New Jersey, joining such aviation legends as Amelia Earhart and Charles Lindbergh. Keith Ferris lives with his wife, Peggy, in Morris Plains, New Jersey, where he maintains a large reference library dedicated to aeronautics.

For information or to order prints, call or write:
Keith Ferris Inc,
50 Moraine Road
Morris Plains, NJ 07950-2750
tel: (973) 539-3363
fax: (973) 605-1863

Roy Grinnell

Capturing aviation history on canvas is Roy Grinnell's forte, and it has brought him worldwide recognition as an aviation artist of the highest caliber. His documentation of aerial combat events has earned him the honor of being the official artist for the American Fighter Aces Association and the Confederate Air Force. In addition, he has done commissioned prints for the Association of Naval Aviation, the Air Force, the National Aviation Hall of Fame in Dayton, Ohio, and the Flying Tigers Association.

Roy's camaraderie with legendary Aces has allowed him to carve an impressive niche in aviation art history in the form of prints and publications. His art has appeared in editions of *Naval Aviation News*, *The Foundation Journal*, *Aviation History* and *The Flight Journal*. He is a member of the Skyhawk Association, the American Society of Aviation Artists, the American Fighter Aces Association, the Confederate Air Force, and the Sino-American Aviation Heritage Foundation, and co-founder of the Institute of Pacific Aircraft Research. Roy was the recent recipient of the prestigious R.G. Smith Excellence in Aviation Art Award, given by the US Navy in Pensacola, Florida.

For information or to order prints, call or write:
Keep Em Flying–Tiger Bay
915 Lower LaCoste Road
Castroville, TX 78009
tel: (830) 538-9775
fax: (830) 931-3696

Jim Laurier

For Jim Laurier, love of art and airplanes have combined to create a fulfilling career. Laurier, graduate of the Paier School of Art in Hamden, Connecticut, has flown a wide assortment of aircraft, lending him extensive knowledge of the ways in which they operate. He is well known for his ability to combine technical accuracy with a realistic depiction of the aircraft in motion. His clients include the U.S. Air Force, the Aircraft Owners and Pilots Association, and *World War II* and *Aviation History* magazines. His work has been exhibited all around the United States, winning top awards at several shows. Dedicated to his profession, he is a Fellow member and Trustee of the American Society of Aviation Artists, and a member of the New York Society of Illustrators, the American Fighter Aces Association, and the Air Force Art Program. Laurier lives in Keene, New Hampshire with his wife, Jill, where he produces electronic art and publishes art prints.

For information or to order prints, call or write:
Aviation Art by Jim Laurier
85 Carroll Street
Keene, NH 03431
tel: (603) 357-2051
fax: (603) 357-4451

Mike Machat

As a teenager, Mike Machat would pour most of his energy and time into his sketches, only to trade them away for a ride in anything that would fly. Destined to become one of America's best-known aviation artists, Machat served as a technical illustrator in the U.S. Air Force before leaving to seek a place in California's aerospace industry. A graduate of California State University at Long Beach, Machat has illustrated and produced many airline histories, including those of Delta, Pan Am, and Aeroflot. His illustrations have led him to work with such clients as Flying Tigers, Continental Airlines, and the Soaring Society of America. Machat's art has won awards in the Illustration West Exhibits and Experimental Aircraft Association Art Competition, as well as the American Society of Aviation Artists' 1992 Founder's Award. His paintings can be seen at the National Air and Space Museum, the Kennedy Space Center, and the Pentagon. A memeber of the American Society of Aviation Artists, the Society of Illustrators of Los Angeles, and the Air Force Flight Test Historical Foundation, Machat lives with his wife Sheri, and their two daughters in southern California.

For information or to order prints, call or write:
Mike Machat Illustration
4426 Desert Drive
Woodland Hills, CA 91364
tel: (818) 591-9433
fax: (818) 591-9495

Stan Stokes

For more than twenty-five years, Stan Stokes has been depicting the world's greatest aircraft. Stokes' attention to detail and his superb illustrative techniques, especially his gift for creating three-dimensional effects, have made a name for the Californian artist. "Incredibly accurate" is a common description of a Stokes painting. His talent not going unnoticed, he received the Benedictine Art Award and First place in the Smithsonian Institution's National Air and Space Museum Golden Age of Flight Art Competition in 1984. His original paintings adorn many of the nation's most famous aviation museums, including the National Air and Space Museum, the Air Force Museum in Dayton, Ohio, and the Museum of Naval Aviation in Pensacola, Florida. From 1985–1991, he produced nine paintings for NASA's art collection. Since 1992, Stokes has teamed up with Bill Deakyne, his publisher and president of the Stokes Collection in Carmel, California, to develop a number of new and exciting aviation art products.

For information or to order prints, call or write:
The Stokes Collection
26352 Carmel Rancho Lane, Suite 105
Carmel, CA 93923
(800) 359-4644

Robert Taylor

Robert Taylor has been painting and sketching since his early years and has earned a reputation that makes him one of today's leading aviation artists. His true talent lies in his ability to take viewers right into a scene, making it almost possible to smell the smoke of battle, or to experience the exhilaration of flight. In the mid-seventies, a noteworthy alliance with the Military Gallery led Taylor on his path to fame. His clients have included the British royal family, a former American president, legendary pilots and aircrews, and other aviation enthusiasts. His work has been featured on television programs and in newspaper and magazine articles. *The Washington Post* described his paintings and drawings as exuding "a lyrical and majestic quality." His one-man exhibition in London in 1983 was heavily covered by international media, as was his one-man exhibition at the Smithsonian Institution's National Air and Space Museum in Washington, D.C., seen by ten million visitors. The latter has been quoted as the most successful aviation art exhibit ever staged.

For information or to order prints, call or write:
Military Gallery/Universal Publishing Group
821 E. Ojai Avenue
Ojai, CA 93023
tel: (805) 640-0057
fax: (805) 640-0059

Nicolas Trudgian

Arriving on the scene in the late 1980s, Nicolas Trudgian is a best-selling aviation artist who has generated artwork for some of the major auto and aerospace manufacturers. Described as a landscape artist who paints aircraft, he enjoys painting the machinery of yesteryear with brilliant colors and resolution. Upon joining the Military Gallery, his paintings were produced as prints for the first time, launching his career on an international scale. Today, the quality of his work is recognized around the world, making him one of the most popular aviation artists in the world. Trudgian lives and works in Gloucestershire, England.

For information or to order prints, call or write:
Military Gallery/Universal Publishing Group
821 E. Ojai Avenue
Ojai, CA 93023
tel: (805) 640-0057
fax: (805) 640-0059

Photo Credits

Index